THROUGH
THE SPANISH PYRENEES
GR 11

Camping below the Anayet lakes (Day 12)

THROUGH THE
SPANISH PYRENEES
GR11: A long distance footpath
'La Senda'

by

Paul Lucia

CICERONE PRESS
MILNTHORPE, CUMBRIA, UK
www.cicerone.co.uk

© 1996 Paul Lucia
Second Edition 2000
ISBN 1 85284 307 1
A catalogue record for this book is available from the British Library

Acknowledgements

I would like to thank my wife for her help in proof reading and
for suffering my many absences whilst acquiring data for this
guide. We still enjoy shorter walks together in the Lakes or
Pyrenees. My thanks too to Rob and Dot Brammall whose timely
arrival at La Guingueta many years ago started me thinking
about backpacking when illness had obliged me to give up
running as a sporting pastime. Seeing a retired couple come into
the campsite with heavy sacks, having walked quite some way
along the GR11 in intense heat, made me think: 'If they can do
that so can I'. Then there are my walking partners, Adrian
Browne and my son Peter-John, who have spent many days and
nights with me in all the weathers that mountains can provide,
leaving us with memories of great times together and firing us
with enthusiasm for yet more adventures ahead. P-J also
accompanied me, during 1999, when we walked the whole route
coast to coast, in the regulation 44 days, earning ourselves a free
beer at Chris Little's bar at Cabo de Creus. Special thanks are due
to Kev Reynolds for his enthusiastic encouragement at the start
of this labour of love and for his advice and help along the way. I
am also very grateful to those who have written to me, often with
up to date information and observations on using the guide.
Particular thanks to Michael Winterton who has written to me at
length of his adventures, imparting valuable facts incorporated
in this revision. Finally, but by no means least, I would like to
mention Jaume Vidal of Espot who has always served me
cheerfully, generously and kindly these past years. I still
remember that he stored dehydrated and trail foods for me many
years ago when he hardly knew me. His welcome was no less in
1999, greeting us with rum and cokes. My heartfelt thanks to all
these who have made this guide possible.

Front cover: Ibón de Llena Cantal and Balaitus (Day 13)

CONTENTS

FOREWORD

In the past thirty years the Pyrenees have been 'discovered' - more than a century after a handful of pioneers from France, Spain and Britain made their sporadic explorations on remote peaks, passes and through deep green valleys.

Thirty years ago mountaineering libraries in the UK contained only a few musty volumes devoted to this magic range. To learn about its history meant delving in obscure journals; deciding from afar what to climb or where to trek during a proposed visit entailed poring over unsatisfactory maps and translating with schoolboy French the guides of Robert Oliver.

But all that has changed and the number of English-language guides and travel books devoted to the Pyrenees is growing in response to a new wave of interest, partly from walkers and climbers weaned on British hills in search of something 'more exotic', or from activists tired of queuing at the foot of an Alpine rock face. As a result of this explosion of interest some of the mystery of the range has gone, but not the magic. Whilst the few previously-known centres have boomed in popularity, and certain barely-known but accessible valleys have achieved a degree of status, there remain vast areas of true wilderness that see few visitors from one year to the next, and romantic, tarn-glistening glens where one could pitch a tent and live in seclusion for weeks of high summer listening to the silence.

Walking the GR11 will reveal some of those special places.

Paul Lucia, author of this guide, has been exploring the Pyrenees for many years and shares my enthusiasm for mountain, tarn and valley. This guide reflects that enthusiasm, and is a product of a number of visits to the Spanish flank where he has followed this little-known but spectacular trail through regions of enchantment. To those who follow I would say: trek with your eyes wide open to the pristine grandeur to be found there, and ensure that it remains untarnished for future generations.

Few will walk the GR11 and not succumb to the spell cast by these mountains. As that great pioneer Henry Russell once wrote: 'It is to the Pyrenees that the smiles of the artist and the heart of the poet will always turn.' So too will the lover of fine wild landscapes. Join the club.

Kev Reynolds

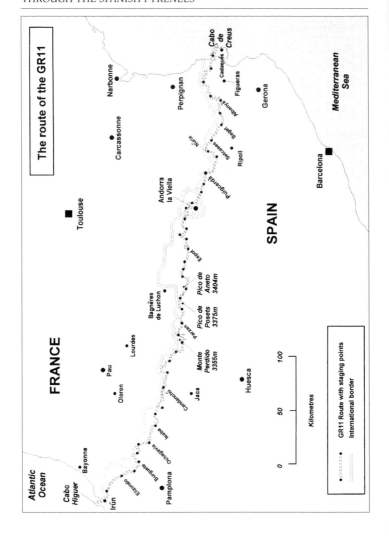

INTRODUCTION

The Spanish Pyrenees present a wonderland to the holidaymaker, whether backpacker, botanist, canoeist, cyclist, entomologist, mountain biker, skier, walker, or simply anyone with a love of mountain scenery, and the chance to enjoy it with much less rain than is usual. This guide will address the needs of walkers either on day trips or on longer expeditions. In recent years the mountain organisations and authorities in the administrative districts of Guipuzcoa, Navarra, Aragón, Andorra and Cataluña have got together with local villagers to arrange the waymarking of a coast to coast (Atlantic to Mediterranean) long distance footpath designated the Gran Recorrido 11, GR11 for short or affectionately 'La Senda', to mirror the French counterpart GR10. This has opened up miles of waymarked footpaths and tracks in an ever-changing environment, often in remote and high areas, to numerous enthusiastic walkers of many nationalities, though the vastness swallows them up so that those seeking solitude will also not be disappointed.

ACCESS

The three main road routes from northern France towards the Pyrenees are: Paris - Bordeaux, Paris - Toulouse and Paris - Perpignan. From these, roads reach the GR11. From west to east these are:

Bayonne - Irún	(day 1)
Bayonne - Irún - Vera de Bidasoa	(day 2)
Bayonne - Cambo les Bains - Puerto de Olsondo - Elizondo	(day 3)
Bayonne - St Etienne de Baigorry - le col d'Ispeguy - Elizondo	(day 3)
Bayonne - St Etienne de Baigorry - les Aldudes - P.de Urkiaga	(day 4)
Bayonne - St Jean Pied du Port - Puerto de Ibañeta	(day 5)
Orthez - Port de Larrau - Ochagavia	(day 8)
Oloron Ste Marie - Arette - le col de la Pierre St Martin - Isaba	(day 9)
Arette - le col de la St Pierre St Martin - Zuriza	(day 10)
Oloron Ste Marie - le col du Somport - Candanchú	(day 12)
Pau - Laruns - le col du Pourtalet - Sallent de Gállego	(day 13)
Lannemezan - St Lary Soulan - Bielsa Tunnel - Bielsa - Pineta	(day 17)
Lannemezan - St Lary Soulan - Bielsa Tunnel - Parzán	(day 18)
Montrejeau - Viella - Viella Tunnel	(day 22)
Viella - Puerto de la Bonaigua - La Guingueta - Espot	(day 25)
Foix - Andorra via Puerto d'Envalira - Arans	(day 30)

Foix - Andorra via Puerto d'Envalira - Encamp	(day 31)
Foix - Latour de Carol - Puigcerdà	(day 34)
Foix - Latour de Carol - Planoles	(day 35)
Perpignan - Prats de Molló - Molló - Beget	(day 38)
Perpignan - Le Boulou - La Jonquera - La Vajol	(day 41)
Perpignan - Banyuls sur Mer - El Port de la Selva	(day 44)

French Rail, SNCF, run excellent services from Paris towards the Pyrenees. Three-day travel passes, valid for one month, include a return Channel crossing starting from Dover. However, planning the best route and being certain of connections requires specialist knowledge and the Travel Agents supplying this service have gradually ceased to do so. It also takes some skill to work out how to get there and back on a three-day pass. Very fast TGV trains and also sleeping accommodation in sleepers or couchettes are available with the payment of a supplement. For a little extra, Eurostar/SNCF combined tickets from London Waterloo can be obtained. Then it is possible to reach the Pyrenees from London within 12hrs, using Eurostar and the TGV. The SNCF part of the ticket must be booked as a return from a specified zone and location only, for the best discounts. This is fine for one or two week holidays, when it is easy to return to the same station from where one started, but for end to end walking of the GR11, one is obliged to book to, say, Bordeaux or Toulouse and then to buy single tickets for the remaining journeys. Please note that it is best to book the return from Cerbère not Port Bou. There is only one through train a day from Port Bou but frequent ones to Cerbère, from where there are many departures northwards. Bookings can be made at Rail Europe, situated just outside of Victoria Station, London, tel: 08705 848848 and at Wasteels, tel: 020 7171 834 7066. I have found that acquiring a recent copy of Thomas Cook's 'European Timetable' together with the small local timetable slips from the railway stations, while visiting the Pyrenees, is most useful for planning rail access. Below is a list of rail destinations with connecting SNCF bus services in italics. All connect with Paris. Only those of interest to GR11 walkers have been included. Taxis can be taken to the road head and thence by foot over the appropriate pass to the GR11 if there is no through road.

Bayonne -	Irún
Bayonne -	St Jean Pied du Port
Pau -	Oloron Ste Marie - *le col du Somport - Canfranc*
Pau -	Oloron Ste Marie - *Laruns*
Lourdes -	*Cauterets*
Lourdes -	*Gavarnie*
Toulouse -	Luchon
Toulouse -	l'Hospitalet - *Andorra la Vella*
Toulouse -	l'Hospitalet - Latour de Carol/Enveitg
Perpignan -	Banyuls sur Mer - Portbou - Llanca

In addition to the above there is also a connecting service between Latour de Carol/Enveitg and Perpignan. The first part of which, in the upper Tet valley, consists of the 'Train Jaune', a narrow gauge railway which can be used to gain access by taxi then foot over high passes to Núria and Setcases.

One of the simplest ways to reach the Pyrenees was by overnight coach from London Victoria. However, the Eurostar/ SNCF combined ticket costs little extra and is so much quicker. Coach travel is still a viable alternative for end to end walks. All coaches have onboard toilets and are non-smoking and have semi-reclining seats. A little care needs to be taken to reduce the discomfort of travelling 20 hours or so in cramped conditions. I have found it essential to have something to cover the eyes and something to stop one's head rolling about. The coaches will stop for meals but sufficient drinks and snacks need to be carried for the whole trip. Eurolines, tel: 0990 808080, run coaches to the following destinations:

Bayonne	Toulouse (connection for Andorra)
Perpignan	Pau
Figueras	Lourdes
Gerona	

The western section can be reached by ferry from Plymouth to Santander and then by coach to Irún. This is especially useful to those living in the West Country.

It is possible to obtain flights to Bayonne/Biarritz, Tarbes (Lourdes), Toulouse, Perpignan, Gerona or Barcelona. These tend to be expensive unless part of a charter. No gas cans can be carried!

EQUIPMENT

It is not necessary here to list in detail the equipment needed by mountain walkers undertaking this route as they would already be well acquainted with the lightest and best kit. Nevertheless, a few comments for those who would like some guidance. First and foremost, I cannot emphasise this too much, **aim for the lightest load possible within the parameters of comfort and safety.** There are two main differences between, say, the English Lake District and the Pyrenees. These are:- 1) It is much dryer most of the time, with the exception of the lower western section, and 2) You can spend more than one day walking up the same hill. This means that heavy loads are much more exhausting, especially if it is particularly hot, and extra quantities of dry clothing are not required as a daily wash will almost always be dry for the next use. A change of underwear, socks and T-shirt will be all that is necessary, though an extra set of underwear and socks will be useful on those rare occasions when washing does not dry. Shorts are the preferred wear though if trousers are to be worn they should be very light. Lightweight boots will be necessary and adequate and trainers or sandals which can be used over easier sections and road walking. Boots are not allowed in most of the manned mountain huts so your own footwear is more comfortable than that which may be provided. As on all mountain walks, waterproofs must be carried. The sun is particularly fierce on northern skins so proper protection will be needed for exposed parts. A hat will be most useful, but make sure that light does not pass through. I have suffered bad sunburn through a hat before I checked this! Lightweight stoves are the order of the day for any cooking. If the preferred fuel is camping gas then spare cans sometimes can be obtained. If re-sealable cans of Butane/Propane mix are used, then these can be purchased only in Benasque, south of the route, and in Andorra la Vella, also south of the route, to my knowledge. A small sturdy tent will afford all the shelter, comfort and flexibility required. Sleeping bags really do require personal research. One has to juggle between weight and warmth for those cold nights at altitude and lightness, perhaps suffering the occasional cold night. It is always advisable to carry at least some water in an easily accessible water bottle, though the text will show when long distances have to be covered without any possibility of replenishment. Further lightweight water containers will be essential in the dryer areas. I use Platypus two and a half litre ones as these take half of a Micropur MT5 tablet, which provides drinking water within 30mins. Food will be of a personal requirement and again the text will indicate if more than one day's supply is needed. Personally, I try to ensure that I have bread, condensed milk, coffee, some soups and maybe a little cheese, as daily essential and emergency supplies. Compass and maps should be carried, of course, the latter inside a waterproof case, just in case of rain, and the certainty of sweat! Please refer to the 'Map' section for guidance. If photographs are to be taken and it is not expected to have them enlarged too much, then a compact perhaps with mini zoom would be ideal, especially now that very light models are on the market with even better lenses. For those who expect to have their masterpieces form large prints, either from slides or negatives, then a SLR or larger will have to be carried, perhaps with tripod, with the extra weight involved. All this, plus individual bits and pieces, will need to fit into a strong rucksack, well tried out beforehand and adjusted for comfort.

FLORA AND FAUNA

Even non-botanists would find it hard not to be moved by the quantity and variety of flowers, often clothing whole mountainsides. Dog tooth violets appearing in the footsteps of the retreating snow. Elderflower orchids showing soon after in their distinctive yellow or purple hues, at first glance looking like clumps of hyacinths. Most people are amazed at the quantity and variety of gentians. The large pendulous heads of the Pyrenean saxifrage decorating small crags also gain immediate attention. For the British, seeing large birds of prey soaring overhead and sometimes below, when on the high ridges, is always exciting. It is possible to see several varieties of vultures. Griffon vultures, often confused with golden eagles at distance, are seen most frequently. Egyptian vultures less so with perhaps rarer sightings of the bearded vulture or lammergeier, distinguished by its large size and pointed wing tips. Red and black kites frequent lower altitudes. Both golden and Bonelli's eagles can also be identified. Carrying field guides while backpacking adds a lot of weight so I usually photograph flowers of interest and make field drawings of any unidentified birds for identification at home.

GEOGRAPHY

The Pyrenean mountain chain can be said to have its beginnings as a rocky promontory on the Atlantic coast of Spain in the south-east corner of the Bay of Biscay and then extending roughly east-south-east some 435 kilometres, as the crow flies, to another such headland on the north-west coast of the Mediterranean Sea. Any walkers' route will almost double this distance. From the west coast it quickly rises to hills of Lake District proportions. Peña de Aia at 806 metres is but 12 kilometres, in a straight line, from Cabo Higuer. In the east, the rugged countryside is not quite so high. Roda at 670 metres is just under 3 kilometres from the coast at El Port de la Selva bay and just over 14 kilometres from Cabo de Creus. The range rises to over 3000 metres in the central part with wooded ridges soon running down northwards to the farmlands of France while waves of seemingly endless sierras sweep south into Spain only arrested by the Ebro river valley of Rioja fame. An exception to this generalism is the delightful high mountain area of the Neouvielle National Park in France, north-east from the Ordesa. However, it is not surprising that the three highest summits are to be found on the Spanish side of the border. Monte Perdido at 3355 metres, Pico de Posets at 3375 metres and Pico de Aneto at 3404 metres therefore attract as much interest from those living north of the divide as those from Spain. Much of the central high ground and watershed is used as the international border between France and Spain. It will be noticed from maps that west of Andorra the high ground of the eastern section passes to the north of that coming from the west, thus forming the valley, Vall d'Aran, which opens to the north-west into France. The two sections are joined at the eastern end of the valley by the high pass of Puerto de Bonaigua, used as a useful road to the south complete with bus route. Another interesting feature of note is that the melt waters of the small Aneto glacier pass underground at the collapsed cave called Forau de Aiguallut (Trou de Toro) and find their way underground, through the intervening ridge, to Vall d'Aran to join the River Garonne flowing into France which passes through Toulouse, turns to the west, to flow into the Bay of Biscay beyond Bordeaux. The Pyrenees being of a lower altitude and latitude than the Alps do not have large areas of permanent snow and ice to limit the activities of walkers. Therefore, more terrain is open to walkers as opposed to alpinists.

GR10 AND GR11 COMPARED

The two routes are similar in the Basque region. Navigation is difficult due to the plethora of trails compounded with the continual improvement and extension of 'pistas' (rough vehicle tracks) for the farming community. As mentioned in the 'Weather' section below, the central and eastern parts of the GR11 become progressively dryer the farther east one goes. The high and hot Spanish plateau to the south keeps wetter weather to the north at bay. There are a number of valleys on the Spanish side which run west/east which reduces the amount of ascent and descent required on the GR11. In the high central area there is less forest on the Spanish side and therefore more exposure to the sun. Both routes try to locate accommodation at the end of each stage. In France this is often achieved by using 'gîtes d'étape' (private hostels). There is no equivalent in Spain, though in recent times it is becoming more common to find local homes offering overnight accommodation. Enquire at the local tourist office or bar.

INSURANCE

Normal holiday insurance should be sufficient to cover basic holiday and medical needs. It is worthwhile shopping around. The demarcation between mountain walking and climbing is the use of a rope, in insurance terms. Most personal holiday insurance now covers hill walking, rambling, scrambling and camping (i.e. activities excluding the use of specialist equipment such as ropes and ice axes). Take the original copy of the insurance with you to the Pyrenees, but leave a copy with a relative or friend at home. Also, check to see if emergency helicopter evacuation is covered. The form E111 should be presented for free basic medical care in Europe.

MAPS

The whole route is covered by the Spanish 'Servicio Geografico del Ejercito' 1:50,000 series, though the trail, as such, is not marked on these. The excellent French 'Randonnees Pyrénéennes' maps, at the same scale, have the path marked, sometimes incorrectly, but unfortunately often do not reach far enough south or the very area required is covered by the key thus making them mostly only suitable for the GR10. The Spanish 'Editorial Alpina' maps, complete with accompanying guide in Castilian Spanish or Catalan, used to cover only the central high mountain section but now they have been improved and their scope extended. These either come in 1:25,000 or 1:40,000 scales. The map or maps covering each stage will be indicated in the text below the introduction to every daily stage. We are unable to publish copies of Continental maps so a sketch map for each stage is provided showing the route in relation to the main geographical features. Notes on these appear under the heading 'Sketch Maps'. It will be necessary to have the relevant map or maps for the sections walked for map and compass work are still very much required on these long distance mountain trails, especially in the lower eastern and western sections. Also, it would be good policy to appraise oneself of the general geography of the area in relation to escape routes both north and south should these become required. Good road maps or the SGE 1:200,000 series maps are adequate for this. However, anyone planning to walk the whole of the GR11 at one time or even a large section of it would be weighed down with maps - though their wallet lightened considerably! It is suggested, therefore, that the Castilian Spanish guide (GR11, Senderos de Gran Recorrido, Senda Pirenaica, ISBN 84-87601-24-3) is also purchased. This is complete with excellent coloured maps at a scale of 1:50,000, published in a loose-leaf format. Even so, there are some glaring errors and attention to these is given in the text. You never know, your local library might obtain it for you.

MOUNTAIN HUTS

These range in quality from hotel standard to bothies used as cow sheds. Information is given in the text concerning usable places encountered on the route. Listed here are the main huts (refugios) along and close by the route which have a guardian(s) resident during the period of opening shown. There is usually a small shelter left open all year alongside or near to the main building, details in text. Opening times are approximate as these are dependent upon snow conditions and other variable factors each year.

El Aguila (day 11)
    Open from June to October - Tel: (974) 37 32 91/37 32 22
Respumoso (day 13) - Open all year - Tel: (974) 49 02 03
Casa de Piedra (day 13)
    Open all year - Tel: (974) 48 71 72
Góriz (day 15)
    Open all year - Tel: (974) 48 63 79
Viadós (day 18)
    Open end of June to beginning of October - Tel: (974) 50 60 82
Estós (day 19)
    Open all year - Tel: (974) 55 14 83
Hospital de Viella (day 21)
    Open all year - Tel: (973) 64 00 18
La Restanca (day 22)
    Open June to end of September - Tel: (933) 02 64 16
Colomers (day 23)
    Open mid June to October - Tel: (973) 64 05 92
Amitges (day 24)
    Open June to October, some spring weekends and possibly
Christmas week - Tel: (933) 15 23 11
Mallafré (day 24)
    Open end of May to November - Tel: (933) 02 64 16
Josep M Blanc (Variant, day 24)
    Open June to September - Tel: (933) 15 23 11
Colomina (Variant, day 24)
    Open 15th June to 30th September - Tel: (933) 02 64 16
Vall Ferrera (day 28)
    Open from June to October - Tel: (973) 62 07 54
Coma Pedrosa (day 29)
    Open 21st August to end of October in first year of opening
(1994) - Tel: (9738) 36 6 13/35 0 36

Estanys de la Pera (Variant, day 31)
    Open July and August - Tel: (937) 83 07 53
Cap del Rec (Variant, day 31)
    Open all year - Tel: (936) 74 53 96
Ull de Ter (day 36)
    Open June to end of September - Tel: (933) 15 23 11

MOUNTAIN RESCUE

There is no voluntary mountain rescue service in the Spanish Pyrenees similar to that in the UK. For any emergency assistance it will be necessary to first reach a telephone or guarded hut and, armed with a map with 'x marks the spot', contact the local Guardia Civil. However, finding a hut with radio or reaching a telephone can involve a long trek. Even though helicopters are now often used to evacuate the injured, rescue could still take some time. Therefore, greater care must be taken to avoid injury or illness. From this it will be seen that, with the distances involved in some areas, a degree of personal commitment is needed over and above that required in British mountains. Actually this adds to the sense of adventure and exploration, so that even in our modern times an element of personal resourcefulness and survival ability can be experienced. There are rescue service numbers appearing in Spanish guides and those relevant are listed below. Bear in mind that mobile telephones do not always work in mountainous areas.

Navarra	Burguete	(948) 76 00 06
	Roncal	(948) 89 32 48
Aragón	Jaca	(974) 31 13 50
		(974) 36 13 50
	Panticosa	(974) 48 70 06
	Torla/Boltana	(974) 50 20 83
		(974) 24 41 24
	Benasque	(974) 55 10 08
Andorra		(9738) 21 2 22
Cataluña	Camprodon	(972) 74 00 15

SKETCH MAPS

There is a sketch map provided for each day. It is hoped that these will greatly reduce the navigation problems that will be encountered. For this purpose, the route is shown in a different format when on a road, pista or path. Roads, pistas and paths not used by the GR11 are also shown differently. No contours are given but spot heights in metres and water courses will indicate the general lie of the land. Where other GR routes cross or pass along the same way, they are labelled for interest. It will be noticed that different print sizes have been used for different labels. Mountain names, spot heights, passes, road numbers and other GR routes use one size in bold. Chapel, bar, farm and house names are in the same size, bold and italic. Rivers lakes and streams use a slightly larger size in italic but not bold. Towns and stage stops are slightly larger, bold and italic. Other differences are quite obvious. Explanation of the symbols and lines used will be found in the Map Key.

TELEPHONE CODES

Most public telephones are connected to the international network. Calls from both France and Spain to the UK now use the same international code. Dial 0044 (then dial the UK number minus the first 0).

WATER

One must decide, on health grounds, the degree of purity of water that can be safely drunk. Therefore these notes are a guide only to assist in this choice. Nearly all high mountain streams have good quality water and I have not had any problems in drinking water from them. However, in the summer cattle are grazed at very high altitudes, therefore, during these months, all water from open sources would be best sterilised. The map must be consulted before taking water to ascertain if there is any form of habitation upstream. Bearing in mind that some refugios use the local stream as a drain/sewer! It is always good policy to take water from side streams anyway. Mountain lakes also can have good quality water but more care is needed. Lower down, due to livestock and farmsteads, all sources need to be treated with suspicion. Cheap bottled water from village stores can solve the problem of drinking water when there are no water points. Water points are noted both in the text and on the sketch maps in these lower areas.

WAYMARKING AND NAVIGATION

The waymark signs are:-

- White horizontal stripe above red on rocks, posts or trees, means the correct route.
- Red and white diagonal cross means incorrect route.
- White horizontal stripe above red with added white directional arrow indicates change of direction.
- Signposts are also marked red and white, labelled GR11, with direction and destination noted.

It is important to be aware that all marking over the whole 800 plus kilometres is done mainly by volunteers in their own time, so spare a thought for them when you also have laboured up some interminable slope to great height to find comforting marks in very remote places. Please forgive them when you find yourself lost (misplaced) and wish that the marks were more frequent. Obviously time will erase any marking and sometimes fresh undergrowth will hide old marks before remarking is carried out. Therefore skill in navigating through forests and mountain landscape will need to be re-enforced with the aid of compass and map. Locating the correct exit from places of habitation is particularly awkward. Help is given in the text. Also please note that:-

1) Often marking along pistas is infrequent.
2) There may not be marks in towns and villages.
3) Marking is missing through most of the Sant Maurici part of the National Park of Aiguestortes and Sant Maurici, except for occasional wooden posts.
4) No marks either on the valley floor of the Ordesa National Park until the Circo de Soasa, though there are numerous other GR11 type marks beyond this.
5) In Andorra there are many GR11 variants differentiated by suffixes on signposts though the route markings are identical and confusing.

In recent years there have been many changes taking place in the Spanish Pyrenees. New ski resorts, campsites and roads ever encroach upon the wilderness. Landowners too require changes to the route of the GR11, frequently just after guides have been put to print! So do expect and prepare for some change to the data contained here. One last, but by no means least, comment concerning navigation. The maps covering this route are not to the standard that we expect from the Ordnance Survey. Sometimes, when trying to triangulate a position, a mountain top will not be found to be in the exact place shown on the map, but extra points of reference solve the problem.

WEATHER

Generally speaking it is much dryer on the Spanish side of the divide, especially in the central and eastern sections, though the lower western section is subject to maritime winds and is much wetter on both sides of the border. By the end of May winter snow can clear sufficiently for safe progress to be made in the higher areas but sometimes passes can still be blocked in mid-June complete with threatening cornices. However, many snow slopes lasting into the summer can easily be surmounted without special equipment, once softened by the morning sun. Occasionally bitter winds can stop this process and the steeper slopes cannot then be climbed without crampons which would force a delay or use of an alternative route.

Frequently, while the GR10 in France is shrouded in morning cloud or mist the GR11 will be bathed in brilliant sunshine warming early starts and adding urgency to gain higher altitudes to assuage the heat of the day.

These balmy days will be very hot in the valleys and storms do develop during the afternoon or evening on occasions, more so as the summer progresses.

A word of warning! The weather in mountainous areas can change rapidly from one extreme to another. Be prepared! Temperatures during storms can plummet to well below freezing even in high summer or raise the temperature to an uncomfortable high. The lowest summer temperature recorded on the top of Aneto, the highest peak in the Pyrenean chain at 3404 metres, is minus 15°C. I have experienced, in early June, 33°C heat at 1300 metres and a week later at 1700 metres endured a snow storm overnight. The previous day, in a bitter wind, standing water and stream edges were frozen at 2100 metres even during the sunshine from a cloudless sky. Overnight, four inches of ice had formed in the washbowl. For the day walker, the possibility of weather change should hold no fears as a rapid retreat to the valley will save the day. For those undertaking longer journeys, suitable kit will be necessary for comfort and safety. Spring months of recent years have tended to be very wet and cold. The backpacker, snug in tent and sleeping bag, will have a warm and comfortable haven in all conditions. On the other hand, those walking the whole route from west to east will, no doubt, encounter very high temperatures during the final week.

WILD CAMPING

Apart from the comforts of proper campsites, the GR11 affords splendid opportunity for wilderness camping. An ideal campsite should have a clean water supply and a reasonably flat, clear, grassy place as backpacking tent groundsheets tend to be fairly fragile. Of these places there are plenty. However, it is very useful to know of the possibility of camping in advance either for planning purposes or if, because of fatigue, threatening weather or for any other reason, a change of plans is required. Therefore, information is contained in the guide to assist in these circumstances. Usually it is not possible to camp above 2400 metres due to the boulder terrain, with the notable exception of an idyllic site beside Ibon de Llena Cantal overlooking the Balaitous Massif at 2450 metres, on day 13 and beside the lake below the Baiau hut, at about 2470m, on day 28. Also, it is difficult to find suitable spots when among the cultivated areas above villages. Camping is not permitted in National Parks. The Mountain Associations of northern Spain have recently introduced a policy of no wild camping at all. In practice, backpackers camped in remote places away from roads or camped for survival reasons (exhaustion, injury or bad weather) are overlooked. The important thing, as always, is to leave no evidence of passing. Rules at mountain huts vary. For example, at Goriz, tents are allowed to be erected during the evening but must be taken down during the day and left flat, if more than one night's stay is anticipated.

GLOSSARY

(A) = Aragón (B) = Basque (C) = Catalan

Abri	Cabin	Carretera	Road
Achar (A)	Narrow pass	Casa	House
Agua	Water	Cascada	Waterfall
Aguja	Needle	Caserío	Farm
Alt	High	Castillo	Castle
Alto	High	Circo	Combe
Arroyo	Stream	Clot	Wide valley
Avenida	Avenue	Col	Pass
Avinguda (C)	Avenue	Cola	Tail
Azul	Blue	Coll (C)	Pass
		Colladeta	Small pass
Baix	Low	Collado	Pass
Balle (A)	Valley	Coma (A)	Combe
Balneario	Thermal baths	Creu (C)	Cross
Baxo	Low	Cuello (A)	Pass
Biskar (B)	Shoulder		
Borda	Farm	Dalt	High
Bosc (C)	Wood		
Bosque	Wood	Embalse	Artificial lake
Brecha	Gap	Entibo (A)	Artificial lake
		Ermita	Hermitage
Caballo	Horse	Espelunga (A)	Cave
Cabana	Cabin	Estación	Station
Cabezo	Small hill	Estazión (A)	Station
Cabo	Cape	Estiba (A)	Summer pasture
Cala (C)	Small bay		above the woods
Calle	Street		
Calm (C)	Bare plateau	Fábrica	Factory
Camino	Clear track	Faja	Ledge
Campo	Meadow area	Faro	Lighthouse
Can (C)	House	Faxa (A)	Ledge
Canal	Canal, narrow valley	Feixa (C)	Ledge
Cap (C)	Small hill	Font (C)	Spring
Capella	Chapel	Fronton (B)	Pelota wall
Carrer (C)	Street	Fuén (A)	Spring

23

Fuente	Spring	Plan (A)	Flat area
Gaina (B)	Summit	Pont (A,C)	Bridge
Glera (A)	Scree slope	Port (C)	Pass
Gran	Large or great	Portella	Small pass
		Prado	Meadow
Hospital	Inn (in the mountains)	Presa	Dam
Hostal	Hostel (small hotel)	Puén (A)	Bridge
		Puente	Bridge
Ibón (A)	Glacial lake	Puerto	Pass
Iturri (B)	Spring	Pui	Peak
		Puig (C)	Peak
Jussa (C)	Low		
		Rec (C)	Narrow valley
Lac (A)	Lake	Refugi (C)	Mountain hut
Lago	Lake	Refugio	Mountain hut
Limpias	Clean	Regata	Stream
Llano	Flat area	Rio	River
		Riu (C)	River
Mas (C)	House	Rivereta	Stream
Mendi	Mountain		
Merendero	Picnic area	San	Saint
Mig	Middle	Sant (C)	Saint
Moli (C)	Mill	Santa	Saint
Monasterio	Monastery	Santuario	Sanctuary
Monte	Mountain	Selba (A)	Wood
Muga (A,B)	Frontier marker	Serra (C)	Mountain range
		Sobirà (C)	High, upper
Negre	Black	Soum	Rounded mountain top
Nord	North	Sud	South
Obago (C)	Dark	Torrente	Mountain stream
Orri	Stone shelter or hut	Tossal (C)	Hill
		Tozal (A)	Steep hill, promontory
Paso	Pass	Tuc (C)	Sharp summit
Paul	Boggy area	Tuca (A,C)	Sharp summit
Peña (A)	Crag		
Pic (C)	Peak	Val (A)	Valley
Pica (C)	Peak	Vall (C)	Valley
Pico	Peak	Valle	Valley
Pla (C)	Flat area		
Placa	Town square		

Risco de San Antón (Kopakarri), 601m, which overlooks
the Endara lake (Day 1)

GR11 DAILY SCHEDULE TABLES

H	=	Hotel or Lodgings	**B/R**	=	Bar/Restaurant
B	=	Bar	**S**	=	Shop for victuals
C	=	Campsite	**T**	=	Telephone
Bk	=	Bank	**Re**	=	Refuge with Guardian
Hu	=	Unmanned Hut or Bothy	**Ca**	=	Camping Area or Wildcamp

The bold type **Location** represents the terminus of the day noted in the left column. Items in *italics* are intermediate points with some sort of facility or just waypoints of note. Times are estimates between locations with a **Total** being the total time for the day. An 'x' indicates that a facility is available. Where there is a Bar/Restaurant the bar column has been left blank even if there is a separate bar or bars present. Water points are noted in the text and on the maps. However, refer to the text, as many of these are totally dry at the height of summer. Note that unmanned huts are often used by shepherds who may lock them to protect their own kit.

Day	Location	Altitude	Time	Total	H	B/R	B	S	C	T	Bk	Re	Hu	Ca
	Cabo Higuer		42m			x		x						
	Irún	5m	1h15m		x	x		x		x	x			
	Endara	240m	3h25m			x								x
Day 1	**Vera de Bidasoa**	56m	2h00m	6h40m	x	x		x		x				
	Collado de Lizarrieta	441m	2h05m			x								
	Gorra	370m	45m											x
Day 2	**Elizondo**	200m	4h25m	7h15m	x	x		x		x	x			
Day 3	**Puerto de Urkiaga**	912m		5h35m										x
	Casa Pablo	840m	2h20m			x						x		x
Day 4	**Burguete**	898m	2h45m	5h05m	x	x		x	x	x				
	Roncesvalles	952m	55m		x	x			x	x		x		
Day 5	**Fábrica de Orbaiceta**	840m	4h05m	5h00m	x	x								x
Day 6	**Casas de Irati**	860m		4h10m		x								x
Day 7	**Ochagavía**	770m		4h35m	x	x		x	x	x				
Day 8	**Isaba**	818m		5h35m	x	x		x	x	x				
	Peña Ezcaurri	2047m	5h00m											
Day 9	**Zuriza**	1227m	1h30m	6h30m	x	x		x	x	x		x	x	x
	La Mina	1250m	4h05m											
Day 10	**Selba d'Oza**	1140m	35m	4h40m		x			x				x	
	Ibón d'Estanes	1780m	4h50m											
Day 11	**Candanchú**	1550m	1h35m	6h25m	x	x		x		x		x	x	x
	Ibones de Anayet	2227m	3h40m											
Day 12	**Salent de Gállego**	1305m	2h30m	6h10m	x	x		x	x	x				

Location		Altitude	Time	Total	H	B/R	B	S	C	T	Bk	Re	Hu	Ca
	Respomuso	2121m	3h25m									x	x	x
	Ibón de Liena Cantal	2450m	1h35m										x	x
	Collado de Tebarray	2782m	1h05m											
	Cuello de Infierno	2721m	15m											
	Embalse de Bachimana Alto	2207m	1h10m										x	x
Day 13	**Balneario de Panticosa**	1640m	1h05m	9h00m	x	x						x		x
	Embalse de Brazato	2360m	2h20m							x				
	Collado de Brazato	2550m	40m											
	Río Ara	2000m	1h10m											x
Day 14	**San Nicolás de Bujaruelo**	1338m	2h40m	6h50m		x			x			x		x
	Puente de los Navarros	1060m	1h15m						x					
	Ordesa Restaurant	1300m	1h00m			x								
	Circo de Soasa	1760m	2h10m											
Day 15	**Refugio de Góriz**	2160m	1h20m	5h45m								x		x
	Collado de Añisclo	2440m	4h00m											
Day 16	**Circo de Pineta**	1290m	3h10m	7h10m	x		x		x	x		x		x
	La Larri	1560m	45m											
	Collado de Pietramula	2150m	2h25m											x
Day 17	**Parzán**	1144m	2h15m	5h25m		x		x						x
	Paso de los Caballos	2326m	3h20m											
	Es Plans	1550m	2h00m						x					
Day 18	**Refugio de Viadós**	1740m	40m	6h00m								x		x
	Plan d'Añes Cruces	2080m	1h10m											x

Location	Altitude	Time	Total	H	B/R	B	S	C	T	Bk	Re	Hu	Ca
Puerto de Gistaín	2592m	1h25m									×		
Day 19 **Refugio d'Estós**	1890m	1h40m	4h15m				×	×	×				
Puente de San Jaime	1250m	1h50m			×								
Refugio de Quillón	1790m	2h20m										×	
Day 20 **Refugio Puente de Coronas**	1980m	1h00m	5h10m									×	
Collado de Vallibierna	2710m	2h50m											
Refugio d'Anglós	2220m	1h55m										×	×
Puente de Salenques	1460m	1h40m											
Refugio de Conangles	1600m	40m							×			×	
Day 21 **Hospital de Viella**	1630m	40m	7h45m		×						×		×
Pòrt de Rius	2355m	1h45m											
Day 22 **Refugio de la Restanca**	2010m	2h25m	4h10m								×		×
Port de Güellicrestada	2475m	1h30m											
Port de Caldes	2570m	1h00m											
Day 23 **Refugio de Colomers**	2115m	1h10m	3h40m								×	×	×
Estany Obago	2236m	50m											×
Port de Ratera de Colomers	2580m	1h00m											
Port de Ratera	2534m	10m											
Estany de Sant Maurici	1920m	2h00m									×		
Capella de Sant Maurici	1880m	10m										×	
Day 24 **Espot**	1320m	1h50m	6h00m	×	×		×	×					
Jou	1306m	1h45m											
La Guingueta d'Aneu	945m	35m		×	×		×	×	×				

Location	Altitude	Time	Total	H	B/R	B	S	C	T	Bk	Re	Hu	Ca
Dorbé	1390m	1h15m											
Coll de Calvo	2207m	2h30m											
Day 25 Estaon	1240m	1h25m	7h30m										
Bordes de Nibrós	1480m	1h00m											x
Coll de Lleret	1830m	1h00m											
Day 26 Tavascan	1120m	2h20m	4h20m	x	x		x		x				
Boldís Subirà	1480m	2h20m											x
Coll de Tudela	2243m	2h00m											
Day 27 Àreu	1225m	2h00m	6h20m	x	x		x	x					
Pla de la Selva	1680m	1h40m											
Sign for Refugio de Vall Ferrera	1840m	1h15m									x		x
Estany d'Ascorbes	2360m	2h00m											x
Day 28 Refugio de Baiau	2517m	35m	5h30m										x
Portella de Baiau	2757m	1h10m											
Refugio de Coma Pedrosa	2260m	1h15m									x	x	x
Arinsal	1466m	1h35m		x	x		x		x				
Col de les Cases	1965m	1h15m											
Day 29 Arans	1360m	55m	6h10m	x	x								
La Cortinada	1340m	15m		x	x								x
Coll d'Ordino	1970m	3h20m											x
Day 30 Encamp	1280m	1h10m	4h45m	x	x		x	x	x	x			
Estany d'Engolasters	1616m	1h05m			x								
Refugio de Fontverd	1880m	1h25m										x	x

Location	Altitude	Time	Total	H	B/R	B	S	C	T	Bk	Re	Hu	Ca
Refugio del Riu dels Orris	2230m	1h15m										x	x
Refugio de l'Illa	2485m	55m										x	x
Coll de Vall Civera	2550m	15m											
Day 31 **Cabana dels Esparvers**	2068m	1h05m	6h00m									x	x
Portella de Calm Colomer	2680m	1h30m											
Refugio Engorgs	2375m	45m										x	x
Day 32 **Refugio de Malniu**	2138m	1h45m	4h00m			x					x		
Saneja	1220m	2h35m					x	x					
Day 33 **Puigcerdà**	1204m	45m	3h20m	x	x		x	x	x	x			
Age	1160m	25m			x		x						
Vilallobent	1170m	20m		x	x								
Collado de la Creu de Maians	2000m	3h05m											
Dórria	1550m	1h45m											
Day 34 **Planoles**	1137m	1h25m	7h00m	x	x		x	x					x
Refugio	1810m	1h45m											
Collet de les Barraques	1890m	15m											
Queralbs	1220m	2h00m		x	x		x		x				
Day 35 **Núria**	1967m	2h30m	6h30m	x	x			x					
Collado de Noufonts	2645m	1h45m											
Pico de la Fossa del Gegant	2805m	45m											
Collado de Tirapits	2791m	30m											
Refugio de Ull de Ter	2200m	1h25m									x	x	
Day 36 **Setcases**	1279m	1h55m	6h20m	x	x				x				

Location	Altitude	Time	Total	H	B/R	B	S	C	T	Bk	Re	Hu	Ca
Collado de Llens	1877m	1h40m											
Molló	1184m	1h40m		x			x		x				
• Collado de la Boixera	1110m	1h10m											
Day 37 **Beget**	510m	2h00m	6h30m	x	x				x				x
Les Feixanes	680m	1h30m											
Collado de Talaixà	760m	2h05m											
Day 38 **St Aniol d'Aguja**	460m	1h05m	4h40m									x	x
Collado de Bassegoda	1105m	2h55m											
Refugio de Can Galan	800m	35m										x	
Day 39 **Albanyà**	237m	2h45m	6h15m	x	x		x	x	x				
La Trilla	700m	2h05m											
St Andreu d'Oliveda	380m	1h35m						x					
Moli d'en Robert	220m	20m			x							x	
Massanet de Cabrenys	340m	55m		x	x		x		x	x			
Day 40 **La Vajol**	515m	2h00m	6h55m	x	x		x	x	x				x
La Jonquera	110m	3h15m		x	x		x	x	x	x			
La Ermita de Santa Llúcia	420m	1h00m											
Puig Falguers	778m	55m											
Day 41 **Requesens**	500m	1h10m	6h20m	x	x								x
Collado de Llosarda	690m	1h50m											
Els Vilars	220m	1h40m											
Collado de Plaja	380m	2h10m											
Day 42 **St Quirze de Colera**	165m	35m	6h15m	x	x							x	x

	Location	Altitude	Time	Total	H	B/R	B	S	C	T	Bk	Re	Hu	Ca
	Vilamaniscle	155m	1h15m											
	Collado de les Portes	230m	1h30m											
	Llanca	15m	45m		×	×		×	×	×	×			
	Sant Pere de Roda	500m	2h05m											
Day 43	El Port de la Selva	12m	1h05m	6h40m	×	×		×	×	×				
	Cala Tavellera	0m	1h55m											
Day 44	Cabo de Creus	15m	2h25m	4h20m		×								
	Total Time	254 hours												
	Total Distance	842 kilometres												
	Total Height Gained	39,455 metres												

*Butresses on the
Alano ridge (Day 10)*

Bahia de Fuenterrabia at dawn (Day 1)

Head of Ara (Day 14)

NOTES ON USING THIS GUIDE

Each stage is given a sequential number and these are listed at the beginning of the book with other useful information. These stages are, of course, quite arbitrary but have been arrived at by use of the traditional benchmark of using places of accommodation. Even so, it is not possible to find shelter at the end of some stages so those without a tent will have to bivouac.

Each day gives a summary of the estimated distance, height gain and loss, and time required. These times are, quite naturally, subjective but are easier to attain than those shown in Continental guides. They have been calculated, and checked on the ground, and are a suitable guide for fit persons able to maintain lengthy days of mountain walking carrying a load of 15-16 kilograms. One advantage of the GR11 is that it often passes through villages where provisions and cheap meals can be obtained, which greatly reduces the weight of food that must be carried. More time than usual has been allowed for the uphill sections, bearing in mind that altitude and load often adversely affect those not acclimatised. Walkers will soon ascertain whether they are going quicker or slower and will be able to adjust these times accordingly.

A profile is provided for each day. Each asterisk indicates the location to which the label refers. Heights are given in metres and distances in kilometres.

The figures in bold immediately in front of the locations noted in the text refer to the cumulative times in hours and minutes for the day. The altitudes given are either the official map heights or are estimated from the maps. Some place names are used from additional sources and will not be found on most other maps but can be located on the sketch maps. Place names used have not been translated i.e. *Collado de* - mountain pass of, but a glossary of terms used has been provided together with a few others that occur on the maps. Those unfamiliar with Spanish or Pyrenean terms will find a working knowledge most useful and the glossary is intended to assist in this direction. The word 'road' in the text refers to a tarmac or concrete road only. For stony or otherwise rough, unsurfaced vehicle track the continental word 'pista' is used throughout. Path, track or trail denote a footpath more or less distinct.

General compass directions given as N = North, ESE = East South-east etc. are to assist in choosing the correct route, especially where there appears to be a choice. Left and right, when in relation to a stream or valley, refer to the true left or right i.e. when looking down the flow. The High Level Route is referred to as HRP both in the text and on the sketch maps, which stands for Haute Randonnée Pyrénéenne.

METRIC CONVERSIONS

To convert *to* metric, multiply by the factor shown. For conversions *from* metric, divide by the factor.

Kilometres	Miles	Metres	Feet
0.5	0.3	100	328
1.0	0.6	300	984
1.6	1.0	500	1640
2.0	1.2	1000	3281
5.0	3.1	1500	4921
8.0	5.0	2000	6562
		2500	8209
		3000	9843
		3500	11483

MAP KEY

GR11 on road	
GR11 on pista	
GR11 on track	
Road	
Pista	
Track	
Motorway	
Power lines	
International border	
Stream	
Railway Line	
Lake	

⟨R⟩	Guarded Refuge
⬠	Bothy
◁	Campsite
△	Wild Camp
H	Hotel
B/R	Bar/Restaurant
S	Shop/Provisions
T	Public Telephone
B	Wayside Bar
W	Water Point
+○	Wayside Chapel
◁	Trig. Point
●—	Daily Start/Finish
▪	House/Farm
. 205	Spot Heights

Day 1: Cabo Higuer - Vera de Bidasoa

Distance:	30.3 kilometres
Height gain:	830 metres
Height loss:	820 metres
Time:	6hrs 40mins

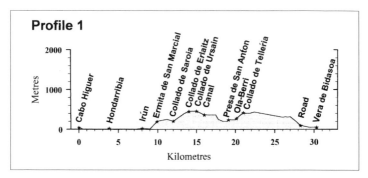

For those who are fortunate enough to have six weeks or so available to walk the whole trail from the lighthouse at Cabo Higuer to Cabo de Creus overlooking the Mediterranean, this must be an exciting time, yet no less exciting for anyone fit enough to start the first part of this varied and entertaining walk. An adventure indeed! Time to exercise mountain navigational skills or to develop them during these lower (by Pyrenean standards) early days through the Basque wooded hillsides. Even the passage through Irún can be borne in the knowledge that one will soon be in the countryside and lost to the frenetic world in which we live even if for only a short while. Food for one day only will be required if it is intended to reach the town at the end of this stage. Please note that the Endara lake is not shown on most maps! Please also note that the route has changed from that shown on the IGN map and previous guides.

Maps: *IGN Carte de randonnées Pays Basque Ouest.*

Camping: *Campsite 'Faro de Higuer', just west of the lighthouse, no longer accepts tents. The two bar/restaurants are still open. There is another site, 'Camping Jaizkibel', 2km west of Hondarrabia. A youth hostel at the northern end of Hondarrabia is recommended. There are*

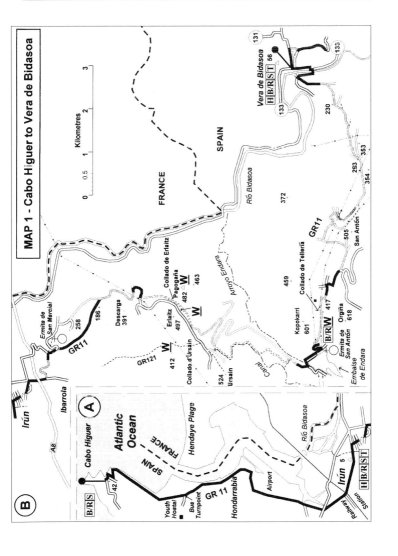

MAP 1 - Cabo Higuer to Vera de Bidasoa

no other suitable places to camp during this day with the possible exception of just below the dam of San Anton beside the pista, where there is a small stream coming off the hillside to the west, although this is a very public place.

The start: Cabo Higuer

0.00 Cabo Higuer, 42m. From the lighthouse go down the road, S, taking the first left down the road with the no entry sign, through the zigzags towards the fishing port, turning right to follow the coast road SSW then S to Hondarrabia. *The mountain seen ahead is Peña de Aia.* Here the road turns from the coast SW to pass the airport leading to the bridge carrying the main N1 road. Pass under the bridge to a large roundabout. The GR11 once turned left here to follow the north side of the main road, without a footpath, but now goes across the roundabout and up the road, Calle Fuenterrabia, SE to the bridge over the main railway line where it curves left, ESE, to pass through the centre of Irún by the main street.

1.15 Irún, 5m. *A large border town geared to tourism.* Pass through the town ESE taking the Paseo de Colón and the Avenida de

Navarra to join the road beside the stream going south to Ibarrola. This means following the street, Paseo de Colón, until it turns slightly left and starts to go downhill. Continue E keeping a look out for a stream passing beneath the road and then take the first street that slants away ESE to the right. In a few metres go across a staggered cross-roads and you should now see a paved pathway to the left of some flats. Follow this path to the road, bearing left, E, over a small bridge to join the Ibarrola road. Turn right, S. *The GR121 markers seen here lead to the Collado de Ursain by the old GR11 route. The new way is slightly longer but much better.* Shortly after, pass beneath the A8 motorway and just before the high tension wires turn left, E, taking a steep stony pista that goes in a long curve left then right to pass beneath the power lines before climbing E with a long section of steps to the left of the track. At a farm the way becomes concrete leading to the road junction above. *The route no longer goes via the Ermita de San Marcial.* Turn right along the road and take the pista on the right at the first bend. This soon becomes a concrete road that leads to a small pass. Turn right, taking the pista that goes up S, curving around the eastern slopes of Descarga, soon climbing parallel to some power lines to the left. Then after a bend with a stream, the pista passes under the power lines to a farm gate. Go through the gate and take the concrete road to the right that climbs first eastwards then westwards to the power lines again. *There is an old path from before the gate that climbs steeply beneath the power lines to this spot, but it is very overgrown.* Just before the cables, turn left, S, up the hillside. Take the right fork, S, by a white building to the road coming up from Ibarrola passing between the two summits of Erlaitz 497m and Pagogaña 482m at the...

3.20 Collado de Erlaitz, 449m. Continue WSW, parallel to the road on its SE side passing a spring, dry in 1999. The track becomes vague and passes over a small grassy lump to...

3.30 Coll d'Ursain, 460m. There is a black and yellow painted post on the right. *Another such post farther along the road indicates the route of the GR121 going down. About 7mins down this track is a good water point with an emergency camping possibility on the left a few minutes before it.* Opposite this first post, take the descending pista SW soon ignoring the path going straight on. *The mountain* *ahead is Peña de Aia, much closer now.* The pista descends in huge zigzags. Turn right WSW, at the next junction and at the next sharp bend where it turns SE, to the right, over a low fence, probably hidden by bushes, will be found a narrow water course and tunnel. *This is the canal carrying water from the Endara lake to Irún. The GR11 follows the concrete edge of the canal for 20-30mins and sometimes the sheer drop to the left, though not large, can be unnerving. It is also very narrow. Those suffering from vertigo should consider continuing down the pista which also leads to the San Antón dam.* Go along the canal edge, against the flow, and after passing a building, about 20mins later, look out for an iron gate on the left with a signpost above on the right. *Here one passes from Guipuzcoa into Navarra.* Go through the gate and follow the path steeply down SE through trees to a small stream. Turn left to join the pista and turn right, SW. *There is the possibility of an emergency camp along this pista by a stream coming from the right.* The pista becomes a road climbing steeply up to the dam.

4.40 Endara (Presa de San Antón), 240m. Turn left across the dam and follow the road to the turning to the bar/restaurant Ola-Berri. Take the road up to the bar with the chapel of San Antón below and have a nice break. Water can be obtained from a hose if the bar is closed. From the west side of the bar take the rough farm track that goes up beside it and climbs E between fields and power lines to reach the...

5.00 Collado de Tellería, 417m. Go down E past the Tellería farm on the left to a cement road which climbs to join another. Turn right, SE, and climb up the cement road which bears left overlooking open fields and other isolated buildings. At the top of the road, as it turns right, carry straight on into the wood along a pista, ESE. In about 500m turn left, at a GR11 no-way mark, and then immediately right. This pista climbs gently to a fork. Bear left and follow the pista N going under two power lines and then take the next gravel pista on the right that turns SE around the summit of San Antón. *The GR11 used to go around the south side of San Antón but now uses the north.* Turn left at the next fork which goes down through a zigzag to join a dirt pista and the occasional waymark. This climbs easily through the wood. Follow the pista to the left of the white building, ESE, contouring the grassy point

354, then going down beneath power lines to a junction...

6.05 a small coll at 293m. Please refer to the sketch map. Do not continue along the pista seen ahead, NE. Find the waymarked old pista just to the left, also ascending NE, at first, beside a fence, not the one on the far left. Avoid turnings right and left. The pista narrows to a track before joining the main pista about 20mins later. Go down left to the road. The road goes down to the river, turn right at the cross-roads and then S to the first old narrow bridge over the river which is crossed and a left then a right turn along a narrow lane leads to the main road. Turn left for the Hostal Euskalduna at the next main turning to the right which is the main street of the rather spread out town of...

6.40 Vera de Bidasoa, 56m. *Hotels, restaurants, shops and telephone and bus service to Irún and to the south. Most services can be found about 600m east.*

Day 2: Vera de Bidasoa - Elizondo

Distance:	30 kilometres
Height gain:	1130 metres
Height loss:	985 metres
Time:	7hrs 15mins

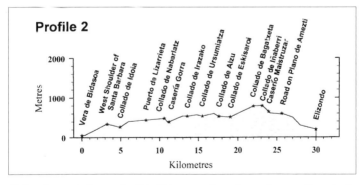

Profile 2

Today the route leaves the Rio Bidasoa and continues in a south-easterly direction gaining high ground and many passes, three of which contain small road crossings, the first at the very border. Then it turns south past the Collado de Inaberri to the Río Baztan and Elizondo. A long day

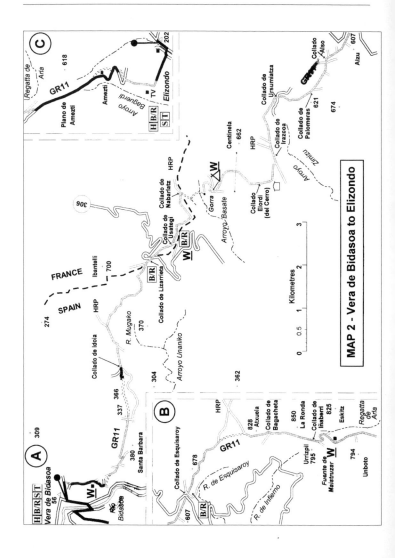

MAP 2 - Vera de Bidasoa to Elizondo

of woodland trails, open ridges and strange and enchanting place names. Please note that the route is incorrectly marked on the Spanish Guide map as it leaves Vera.

Maps: *IGN Carte de randonnées Pays Basque Ouest. SGE 25-5, 25-6 and 26-6.*

Camping: *There is a suitable place south of the farm Gorra.*

0.00 Vera de Bidasoa, 56m. Turn eastwards along the main road beside the Hostal. About 300m later, turn right at an open square, S, to climb a gravel covered pista, ignoring another climbing to the right, passing the swimming pools seen to the left. Just above the pools the pista is joined from the right by the other road that climbs from the south side of Hostal Euskalduna. Follow the road upward, S, to the farm called Migelteneko-borda. Water point. Go up a stony path SE which becomes grassy and is joined by a farm pista on the left. Go up the pista and look out for a sharp turn left, NW, which goes up steeply and soon continues SE again becoming grassy and almost level. Ignore another grassy pista going right which goes to the summit of Santa Barbara where you would find a GR11 waymark. Follow the pista towards a small pass on the east ridge of Santa Barbara...

0.50 ridge, 337m. *Foresters have removed the conifer wood on the hill ahead. It is possible to turn right going steeply down the pista to join with another winding and climbing to the next pass.* However, follow the pista, E, through the debris of the old plantation, aiming to meet the fence line just to the right of the small hill, point 366, where a gate allows access into the fields beyond. Cross the fields by gate and stile to a gate to the right of the farm 'Larrete-Enea' where a grassy track then concrete road go down to...

1.15 Collado de Idoia, 268m. *The narrow road going back to the left, NW, goes to Vera.* Go up the new pista, with Ibantelli ahead, past white farm buildings to a signpost marking the junction with the high level route. Turn right, SE, and climb this pista easily around the SW and E faces of Ibantelli to reach the frontier with road crossing and bar/restaurant at...

2.05 Collado de Lizarrieta, 441m. Frontier marker No.44 in the vicinity. Cross the road and follow a large pista that goes up SE beside the border on the French side, passing a path to the right going down to another bar/restaurant Usategi to reach the Collado de Usategi or Palomeras, 470m, frontier marker No.46. The pista continues to marker No.50 and...

2.30 Collado de Nabarlatz, 477m. *The High Level Route continues along the pista.* The GR11 turns SSW going down a path over grass which shortly leaves this path to turn sharp left, SE, going down to the Basate stream. Cross the stream, then slightly to the right there are two paths. Take the left one climbing S to the farm...

2.50 Casería Gorra, 370m. Go up the pista, SE, which turns to the right to join another coming from the left. Signpost. Turn sharp right, NW, following this pista round to the south again. Shortly, take a left branch SE which passes by a water point and possible spot for the tent. Follow this pista as it makes a sweeping curve around Centinela over the pass of Cerro 550m, past a new unamed refugio to join a pista from the right continuing ENE to...

3.40 Collado de Irazcoa, 530m. Shortly the High Level Route takes the left branch while the GR11 takes the right branch continuing ENE ignoring another branch shortly going off to the left. Go along the left of the ridge, ENE, with the Solaberriko-Turria valley on the left and the Zimizu to the right until a...

3.50 Highpoint, 570m. The pista turns SE crossing the ridge and goes down to the...

3.55 Collado de Ursumiatza, 530m. Cross the little road and go up the pista S then SE to...

4.10 Collado Palomeras, 610m. Go down SE, passing the Collado Also, 530m, where the pista on the left of the ridge ahead is taken, SE, contouring the NE side of Alzu. This leads down to another road crossing at...

4.35 Collado de Esquisaroy, 518m. *The pista going down right goes to the bar/restaurant Esquisaroy.* Cross the road and climb steeply SE by an old deeply eroded pista. The gradient eases as the trail wanders SE above the Esquisaroy valley to a fork by a small iron cross on a wooden post (the post may now have rotted away) where the High Level Route bears left along the pista while the GR11 bears right up a path to the right of the ridge. It then goes down to join a pista coming from the left. Continue southwards along this pista, more or less level, passing the small pass of...

5.20 Collado de Bagacheta, 793m. Follow pista SSW to...

5.35 Collado de Inaberri, 795m. *The pass between La Ronda to the NE and Urrizpil to the SW.* Continue along the pista which goes down southwards through a beech wood, with Urrizpil on the right, to a clearing. Take the left fork of the grassy pista to a zigzag, not many waymarks from now on. Then S and SSW to reach a building with a spring nearby called the Fuente de Maistruzar. Go down by the pista, SSE, which is rutted and scattered with boulders with the upper Arla stream to the left. About 15mins later take the turning to the right which goes up SW a short distance before turning left to meet the new road at a picnic area...

6.15 Plano de Amezti, 580m. *The road here goes along to the hill of the same name then down by zigzags to Elizondo. The GR11 takes short cuts across the loops down the obvious south ridge.* Turn left and continue down along the road to the small hill ahead called Amezti, 627m. Just before the road rises to the top of the hill beside a white house, bear left across rough ground to find a track going southwards, below and to the left of the house, down to the road again. If the track is overgrown, or there is shooting heard, just follow the road to the next section. Turn left, go around the bend to a short-cut going off left once more. The track goes down to and across the road to a pista, though the wood to a wooden gate. Turn left SE along the pista becoming a road going past the telephone relay station, then the school and clinic of 'Nuestra Senora del Pilar', to the SW end of main road through...

7.15 Elizondo, 200m. *Hotels, bars, restaurants and shops. Information office open only in the summer. Non-resealable gas cans available. Turn left, just before the river to find accommodation, with use of kitchen, at Casería Salias.*

Day 3: Elizondo - Puerto de Urkiaga

Distance:	19 kilometres
Height gain:	1050 metres
Height loss:	340 metres
Time:	5hrs 35mins

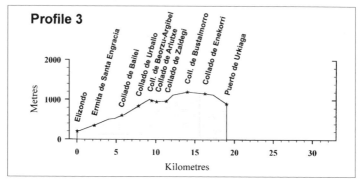

Today, for the first time the route tops 1000 metres. Walk the border ridge for a kilometre, enjoying beech woods and grassy ridges. As always, care must be taken with navigation and mist will make it easy to become disorientated. However, the 7km of high ridge from leaving the border to Collado de Enekorri has a fence to guide the way. Some slopes could be slippery in rain. There are no lodgings available for this stage so a camp or bivouac will be necessary around the final pass. Two days' provisions will be required.

Maps: *SGE 26-6.*

Camping: *Wild camping by the Puerto de Urkiaga with water at the locked cabin or use a suitable wartime bunker up the pista of next day's stage. There is also the possibility of a camp just over the Urballo pass.*

0.00 Elizondo, 200m. Leave the town by the Avenida Monsenor Mauricio Berecochea, SSE, on the SW side of the large church. Go up the road for about 500m where it turns to make a large curve to the left. Go straight on, signpost pointing the way, until the road is met again which is followed to...

0.35 Ermita de San Engracia, 354m. Here it becomes a pista climbing towards the SSE. Within a kilometre it turns towards

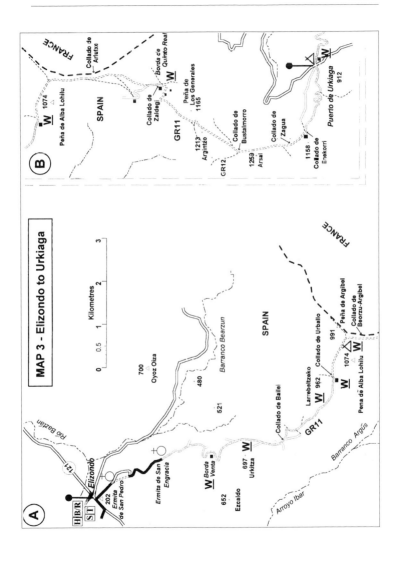

MAP 3 - Elizondo to Urkiaga

the south, then makes a sharp right zigzag to gain height just before the farm 'Borda Venta' over on the right. Continue along the pista, SSE then S, to...

1.35 Collado de Bailei, 606m. Here the pista turns SE. Avoid the turn to the right going SW but go straight on, SE, soon taking the left fork. This goes up the left side of the ridge ahead a short distance before crossing to the right side to continue climbing SE then E to...

2.30 Collado de Urballo, 890m. Situated between Peña de Alba to the SE and Larrebeltzeko to the NW. Hunters' cabin to the right with spring. Here the pista ends. Go straight ahead over the grass ESE to just before a fence where the trail turns right, S, passes through some trees, and climbs to...

2.50 1000m contour. *Camping possible, with water from a small stream. This was in thick cloud the first time that I passed this way and I got accidentally shot at. The shot passed harmlessly over my head and I continued, singing loudly.* Follow the frontier ridge and fence S to, first, Collado de Beorzu-Argibel, 960m, then along the narrow part of the frontier ridge to Collado de Arlutxe, 936m. Avoid a number of tracks descending SSE. Soon the frontier turns to the left but the GR11 carries on S down to join a rough pista coming from the right which goes to...

3.35 Collado de Zaldegi, 947m. *Hunters' cabin to the right with stone tables and benches.* The GR11 goes up to the higher of the two huts above, turning north for a short while before turning left to gain, above the rough ground, the north flank of Peña de Los Generales, 1165m, climbing SW up steep grass, turning south to cross the fence coming down from the summit at its lowest point. Continue SSW contouring Argintzo, 1213m, over on the right, to join the fence again at...

4.25 Collado de Bustalmorro, 1180m. *The GR12 joins here from the right.* Continue S contouring the east side of Arsal, 1259m, to the next pass, Collado de Zagua, 1170m. Continue S over the grass, the shooting hides on the left, towards the little hill ahead. The fence on the right begins to turn towards the east. Then look out for a gate in it with hunters' cabin amongst the trees on the other side. This is...

4.50 Collado de Enekorri, 1140m. Pass through the gate to the beginning of the pista, called Camino Forestal a Zuraun, which is followed SE then E, through several zigzags, all the way down to the road at the pass...

5.35 Puerto de Urkiaga, 912m. Chains usually at the entrances of the pistas. *Water behind nearby hut on east side of the road. Notice board with footpath map. About 7km to the north the road passes into France.*

Day 4: Puerto de Urkiaga - Burguete

Distance:	16 kilometres
Height gain:	680 metres
Height loss:	695 metres
Time:	5hrs 05mins

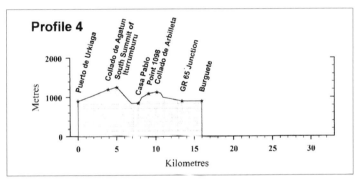

Another day of grassy high ridges, fence lines and beech woods. The need for navigation care required and again mist would make this much more difficult. Rain will make some slopes slippery.

Maps: *SGE 26-6 and 26-7*

Camping: *Barranco Odia or around Casa Pablo. There is a campsite 2km south of Burguete.*

0.00 Puerto de Urkiaga, 912m. Take the stony pista E which climbs through the wood with many bunkers offering refuge in bad weather. About 25mins later take the right fork of the pista

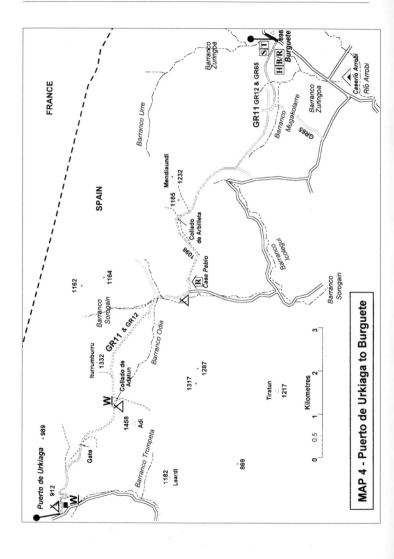

MAP 4 - Puerto de Urkiaga to Burguete

which ends at a metal gate. Go through the gate and follow the track to the SE. The trail contours around the north face of Adi, 1458m, turning towards the east, through a patch of trees to...

1.10 Collado de Adatun, 1200m. A large grassy area. The crag ahead is passed on its north side. Go down a little across the grass, E, to locate a large and clear waymark indicating the start of the ascending traverse of the rocky slope through the wood. Take great care in the wet as this rock is very slippery and precipitous in places. The waymarks lead upward, with the ground becoming easier, out of the wood and up to the west ridge of Iturrumburru (called Collado de Iturrumburru), 1230m. Follow the fence up to...

1.35 Iturrumburru south, 1300m. Here the fence line from Adi to Iturrumburru is joined by one going down SE towards the Barranco Sorogain. Turn SE, going down steeply by the fence which soon vanishes, with the wood to the right. The simplest way from here is to go down SE following the crest of the rounded ridge over very steep grass, broom and bracken, making zigzags as necessary, eventually reaching the little valley of the Odia some 200m from the confluence with the Sorogain. *The GR11 follows the edge of the wood, very slippery in the wet, goes into it for a short while and then goes down the lower slopes without path to the Odia also.* Turn E along a grassy pista to cross the Sorogain stream to the new pista. Turn right, S, and follow this pista to...

2.20 Casa Pablo, 840m. *A road going south starts here.* **Casa Pablo has been extended and now offers full refugio services.** *It is possible to camp nearby.* From the north of the building, take the path eastwards, over a stile, going up to the ridge ahead The waymarks are followed ESE steeply to the ridge and fence above. Turn left at the fence, NE, to continue climbing steeply to point 1098m where the gradient eases. Follow the fence upward. Soon, clear waymarks on a fence post are seen. It is possible to cross here and follow the track parallel with the fence but it is better to continue easily upwards, with the fence on the right, NE then W to...

3.20 Collado de Arbilleta, 1135m. The fence continues to Mendiaundi but the GR11 crosses it by a stile here to go down a grassy track SSE and in a couple of minutes cross another fence to a pista which is followed SE steeply down through the beech woods. This is covered with sand after the sand quarry. About 2km later this is joined, from the right, by a newer pista which is followed SE. In just over another kilometre the pista turns left to a well marked tree at the corner of a wood with open arable land ahead. Turn right and follow the edge of the field to the right. At the last corner the St. James of Compostela route, GR65, with yellow markers, joins from the south through a gap in the hedge. Turn left along the edge of the field where the track widens, passes into a wood, crosses two small streams to gain a narrow passing place giving access to a large pista which eventually goes past farm buildings (left), then a footbridge over the Barranco Zuringoa. The steep stony road leads to the main road through...

5.05 Burguete, 898m. *Turn right for Hostal/Restaurants. Turn left for supermarket just down left from the main road at the next junction with telephone booth opposite. Hotels, bars, restaurants, shops and Youth Hostel. The road going north reaches the border with France then on to St.-Jean-Pied-du-Port. Go 2km south to Camping Arrobi. NB. Fresh bread only arrives at the panadería after 11am.*

Day 5: Burguete - Fábrica de Orbaiceta

Distance:	20.5 kilometres
Height gain:	600 metres
Height loss:	660 metres
Time:	5hrs

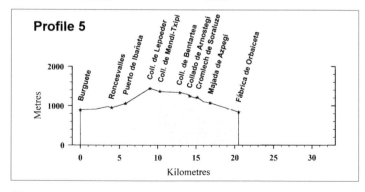

From Burguete the trail passes through farmland then woods to Roncesvalles with its large abbey founded as a stop over for pilgrims on their way to Santiago and still used for this today. On to Puerto de Ibañeta, often in cloud, before climbing to the high ground of Astobiska, turning south down a pista to the old munitions factory Fábrica de Orbaiceta. The high area tends to be wet with low cloud, so care will be needed with navigation. Provisions for three days will be required.

Maps: *Editorial Alpina Roncesvalles.*

Camping: *Along the river north of Fábrica de Orbaiceta. There is a better place on a grassy shelf above the pista beside the barranco Txangoa. Also, near to the water point at border stone 205, though rather public.*

0.00 Burguete, 898m. Take the road WNW down past the supermarket crossing the Barranco Suringua. Ignore a pista to the right. About 300m from the town, at an open grassy place, turn right, N. Ignore GR11 marking ahead which would take you left around farm buildings to yesterday's stage but go N. Avoid taking either the road or the pistas on the left but cross a small stream by a narrow footbridge and continue N. About 20mins from town, go through an iron gate and very soon take a grassy pista NE, gaining access through a barbed wire hurdle into the wood. The top of the hurdle can be lifted off. Continue generally NE passing an open area and junction. The pista joins a cement road coming from farm buildings on the right, which climbs a short way to the N, then turns E to meet the main road at a sharp bend. Turn right, down to...

0.55 Roncesvalles, 952m. *Accommodation, meals and Tourist Office. An important monastery on the pilgrim route.* Either follow waymarks into the monastery courtyard and find a way to the pista behind the buildings, gate at start, or, pass around the buildings to the south and turn left down to the pista. Follow the pista N, taking a wide trail on the left, sign-posted 'Ibañeta', to...

1.20 Puerto de Ibañeta, 1057m. *Here there is a monument to Roland and a GR11 signpost. The HRP joins from the W. The Lepoeder pass can be reached by walking up the narrow road going E. It can be avoided by a harder climb NE along the ridge.* Take the narrow road E for a few minutes until the first large curve to the right where

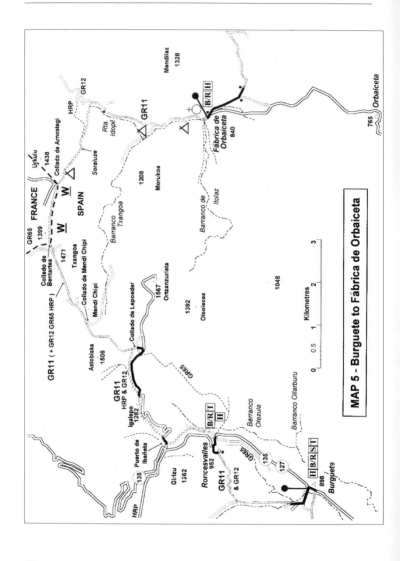

MAP 5 - Burguete to Fábrica de Orbaiceta

waymarks indicate a narrow track on the left climbing NE. The trail passes Igalepo off to the left, arriving at a grassy pass near the road. Take to the road here and climb easily to a short cut on the left which climbs to...

2.20 Collado de Lepoeder, 1445m. *The GR65 coming from Roncesvalles joins from the S at the short cut and so, all friends together, the GR11, GR12, GR65 and HRP unite for a while. The summit of Astobiska, 1506m, can be reached to the N in about 20mins but steps have to be retraced to join the GR again, though it is possible in clear weather to come down the steep NE ridge to the Collado de Mendi Chipi.* Take the pista that goes down N and then turns NE to contour the SE side of Astobiska to reach, on the NE ridge...

2.40 Collado de Mendi Chipi, 1360m. *The pista going down sharply to the right also goes to the destination for the day and is a very pleasant walk.* The GR11 crosses to the northern side of the ridge and continues ENE along a relatively level pista of Roman origin, avoiding a pista going up right and another going down to the left as the route passes below the summit of Mendi Chipi and Txangoa. At a junction about 150m after leaving the wood with a ladder stile over a fence ahead, the Compostela trail turns left while the GR11 takes the right fork for a few metres before turning off left, E, to cross the fence by another ladder stile just S of the first one. This is the...

3.05 Collado de Bentartea, 1337m. *Frontier between France and Spain, border stone no. 200.* Follow the frontier E then ESE by a vague grassy pista with the fence line to the right. Look out for border stone no. 201, for below, S, is an important water point easily seen and ideal for a lunch break. Continue along the N side of the fence, though one can use the water point side, to the marker stone 205 and...

3.35 Collado de Arnostegi, 1236m. *Over on the left, on the summit of Urkulu, are the remains of a Roman watchtower. The road to the left comes from St.-Jean-Pied-du-Port which makes this pass popular, especially at weekends.* Leave the frontier ESE by a grassy track above the steeper slope with a more obvious grassy track below. Just over one kilometre later the track passes to the left of some large stones identified by a sign as the Cromlech of Soraluze. The track goes down E and very shortly leaves the clear trail *(the HRP* *continues straight on here)* for a track on the right, waymarked, going across fields to the river and pistas below to the area...

4.10 Majada de Azpegi, 1075m. *The GR12 goes N.* Cross the stream by the bridge and follow the main pista S, soon avoiding a pista to the left. The pista from Collado de Mendi Chipi joins from the right in just under 2km. Look out for camping spots if it is intended to camp as there are no suitable places after the Fábrica until 30mins into next day's stage.

5.00 Fábrica de Orbaiceta, 840m. *A group of buildings next to the old armaments factory. There is a bar, the Ostatu Urkulu, where meals can be obtained. Accommodation may be available at the Casa Ruales near the bar. If not, it will be necessary to camp nearby. Accommodation and a meal may be had at the village of Orbaiceta, 4.7km south by road.*

Day 6: Fábrica de Orbaiceta - Casas de Irati

Distance:	16.5 kilometres
Height gain:	400 metres
Height loss:	380 metres
Time:	4hrs 10mins

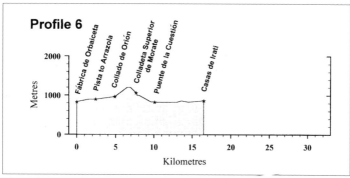

A much easier day allowing a detour to the summit of Mendi-Zar for a panoramic view, if one so wishes. The route climbs the Regata de Arrazola to the southern flank of Mendi Zar before descending the Morate valley to touch the border, then south to the large man-made lake of Irabia. The pista then continues to the camping area at the end of the stage.

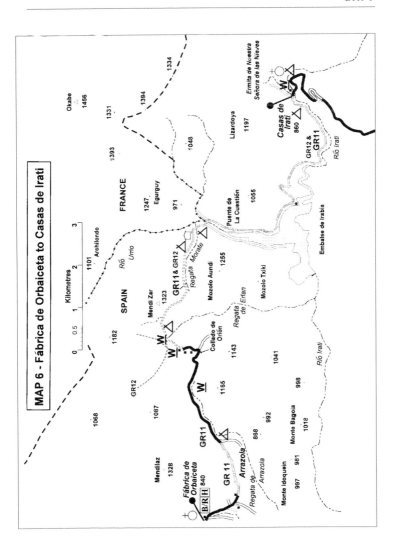

MAP 6 - Fábrica de Orbaiceta to Casas de Irati

Maps: *Editorial Alpina Roncesvalles.*

Camping: *At the head of the Regata de Erlan. Lower part of Regata Morate and Casas de Irati. Other possibilities indicated on the map. The camping area shown on the Spanish Guide map at the head of the Arrazola stream has a no camping sign and any water in the stream is likely to be polluted due to cattle grazing here.*

0.00 Fábrica de Orbaiceta, 840m. Ascend the cement road, E, beside the bar. In about 10mins or so take the left fork to a farm where the trail continues as a pista, E, along the right side of the Regata de Arrazola gradually turning to the NE. The road from Arrazola joins from the right. *Camping is just possible here. The only water is from the stream below and will need sterilising. If it is dry, water can be obtained from Arrazola 500m to the south.* After 2km the road turns ESE then with a left and right turn it arrives at the...

1.10 Collado de Orión, 970m. Take the road that goes up N. *The next section is tricky to navigate!* Just below the second building on the left, take a track on the right, which goes down past a cabin and water point. From here ascend the track NE which joins with the GR12 again as it comes from the left. Another water point is reached at the head of the Regata de Erlan where it may be possible to find sufficient level grass to camp. Continue ENE towards the summit of Mendi Zar as a guide, keeping above the tree line to the right. There are several tracks contouring the south of Mendi-Zar. Keep to the one nearest the tree line. *The upper one reaches the ridge ahead at some rocks with clear waymarks but these lead nowhere. The entry point for the descent through the wood is about 100 metres below, in distance. If in cloud and the rocks are located, either go steeply down the ridge, or go steeply down through the wood using the first small valley to the E of the ridge until the GR is located.* The track gradually turns SE to contour the south flank of Mendi-Zar before crossing the grassy ridge with two isolated and faintly waymarked trees called at...

2.20 Colladeta Superior de Morate, 1060m. *From here a steep climb to the top of Mendi Zar can be made in about 30mins returning by the same route.* Go down E into the wood. Look out for the waymark on a tree indicating the entrance point. Go down steeply through the wood watching out as the GR turns NE just before the streams. Cross a stream and follow the path down SE, about 10-15m above the Morate stream seen on the right. This leads to a grassy pista, which passes a hut to the left, suitable for overnight shelter, and many places to camp. Follow the pista to cross the Morate stream turning right, S, to reach...

2.55 Puente de La Cuestión, 825m. Cross the bridge turning S along the pista beside the lake, Embalse de Irabia. Much later, avoid a turning to the right going down to a private cabin but turn left, NE, and climb the pista leading to various loops and bends, which take you to the Río Irati which then is followed eastwards along its right bank to a bridge which crosses the river to join the road end from Ochagavia below the ruins of...

4.10 Casas de Irati, 860m. *A camping spot can be found by taking the path to the chapel and then, below the chapel, turn right down a wide track into a field with a water point.*

Day 7: Casas de Irati - Ochagavia

Distance:	16 kilometres
Height gain:	670 metres
Height loss:	760 metres
Time:	4hrs 35mins

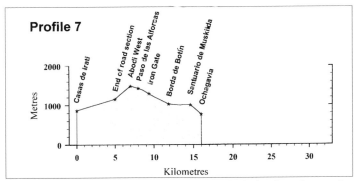

This stage goes generally southwards, through the lovely and extensive forest of Irati, crossing the Abodi ridge, with splendid views in every direction. Lodgings and provisions at the end of the day. The GR11 has been re-routed a number of times to avoid the 5km road climb from the

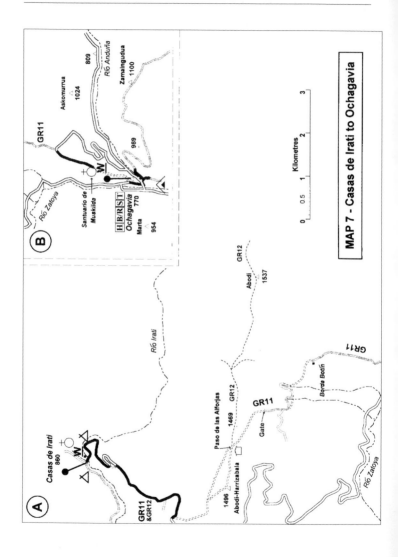

MAP 7 - Casas de Irati to Ochagavia

Casas de Irati to the ridge that gives access to Abodi. Due in part to old markings, I have been unable to map the present route. Some parts are extremely steep and slippery and are not inviting. Other clearly marked parts become unclear. There is little traffic on the road, so I suggest using the road except for the short cut across the first big zigzag. Navigation could be tricky in cloud especially finding the route off the side of the Abodi ridge. NB: There is no certainty of any water today until Muskilda so sufficient water will need to be carried.

Maps: *Editorial Alpina Roncesvalles.*

Camping: *Camping Osate, 500m south of Ochagavia on the east side of the river. It's best to cross the bridge over the Río Anduña to the main square. Exit the square by opposite corner to locate new road passing by new buildings to the camp. 5min slow walk. Open all year (except Nov).*

0.00 Casas de Irati, 860m. From the bridge go up the road, E, which curves round to the W then SW. At the bend which doubles back NE, go steeply up though the wood, S, to join the road again shortly. Continue along the road SW then S. *At the 20km marker there are clear waymarks to the right but I could not find all the route.* Continue along the road until the 19km marker and then look out for waymarks on both sides of the road just as it turns left crossing a small ridge. Turn left here, S, and climb steeply a clear track, very slippery when wet, through the forest. About 1km later at the edge of the wood, by an old fence, the route turns left, E, to follow the fence line to a snow depth pole on the open mountainside. There is no clear trail here but one appears about 100 metres from the post on the route to the pass. The trail passes just above a line of trees. In cloud, the pass can be identified by the two large sinkholes. Go round them and bear just east of south to the pass and hut. So, ESE will take you directly to Paso de las Alforjas or SE directly to the east summit (just to the left of the skyline rocks but not seen) of...

2.10 Abodi, 1496m. The view is well worth the visit in clear weather. Follow the grassy ridge E to the wide grassy pass of Alforjas, 1440m. Signpost was on the ground in 1999. *The GR12 continues E from here.* Go down S over grass by a vague path to a shepherds' hut with two rooms in good condition. From the hut go E at first, keeping above the steeper ground, then SE above the woods. About 10-15mins from the pass look out for an iron gate in the fence below, turning S down a grassy ridge to reach it. Go though the gate and follow the grassy pista S to a clear pista turning E. Shortly follow waymarks across grass to the right, down to the stream. Climb back to the pista above and at the gate continue straight on, with gate and fence on the left, to the second stream. Cross this and follow the rocky path S then SE through bushes to the edge of the wood and...

3.25 Borda Botín, 1030m. Take the pista SSE along the ridge turning S to join the road coming up from the left and Ochagavia. Turn right and follow the road SSW to...

4.05 Santuario de Muskilda, 1010m. *Water point and picnic area.* Pass through the sanctuary or pass by on the right if the gate is locked and on the other side go down the steep steps and old cobbled path, SSW, all the way to the cobbled streets of Ochagavia. Bear left down through these to reach the centre of...

4.35 Ochagavia, 770m. *Hotels, restaurants, lodgings, shops and bank.*

Day 8: Ochagavia - Isaba

Distance:	23.8 kilometres
Height gain:	710 metres
Height loss:	655 metres
Time:	5hrs 35mins

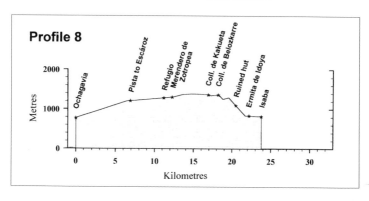

An unusual day in that one could go all the way to Isaba on the same pista, though the GR11 descends through the woods by a different route. It is also a dry day so water will need to be carried especially as there is no shade above the forests. There is a hut for shelter about half way but no water. The pista climbs gently through the woods east of Ochagavia to follow wide ridges to pass around the north face of Kakueta before taking a complex but well marked route down to Isaba.

Maps: *Editorial Alpina Roncesvalles.*

Camping: *There are no suitable camping spots due to the lack of water.*

0.00 Ochagavia, 770m. From the main square go to the River Anduña and take the cobbled street NE on the south side of the river to a building showing an 'Exposition' sign. Pass between it and another showing 'Estación de Patatas'. Follow the road right then left which becomes a pista ascending NE. This climbs and turns back above the town before turning E. It is easy to locate one's position along this long route by the direction of travel and reference to the sketch map as the route changes direction quite distinctly from time to time.

1.50 Junction with pista to Nebazkene and Ezcaroz, 1210m. Continue SE. Some time later avoid a pista to the right but take the one turning NE. Much later the pista makes a loop to the north, passing a hut to the head of a valley. There is also a hut here but no water. Then it heads SE to...

2.45 Merendero de Zotropea, 1300m. *A picnic area with GR signpost and junction with the GR13.* Ahead, SE, one can either take the pista or go over the grassy hill. Both rejoin to pass to the right of Lakuaga Sierra, 1415m, continuing along the ridge to the north face of Kakueta which is contoured to finally climb NE to...

3.45 Collado de Kakueta, 1365m. Here the pista turns sharp right, S, to contour the E of Kakueta. The GR11 has been re-routed. Turn left, N, and follow the earthy pista down to a sharp bend to the left above a small grassy saddle seen close below. Look to the right and waymarks and a clear path will be seen gently ascending the side of the hill over grass. This joins another earthy pista. Continue E taking the right branch in a few metres which climbs a short way to...

4.00 Collado de Belozkarre, 1370m. Look out for the marks

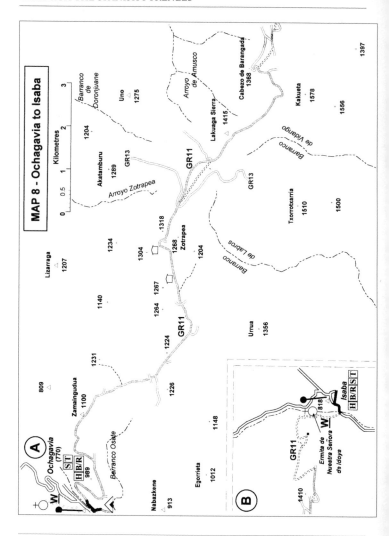

MAP 8 - Ochagavia to Isaba

Central gully, Peña Ezcaurri (Day 9). Not as steep as it appears

directing you to go down yet another earth pista to the right and almost immediately turn left down a path through the trees following the marks E down to the earth pista a short distance below. Go E down the pista for about 5 minutes and where the bank on the left comes down to the level of the pista, keep a look out for waymarks where a faint path is taken sharp left, NW. This curves around the head of a small wooded valley, crossing two streams, before heading ESE again. Then it goes down a ridge, take care to take the right branch (it might be possible to spot the very faint 'no-way' marker on the left branch), which goes to a ruined building where another sharp left is taken NNW through the bushes to find the path and waymarks leading down and turning E. Take care to locate the waymarks on this steep descent which keep to the left of the more obvious routes down through the small trees, sometimes following a fence line seen to the left, to a change of direction marker on a tree indicating a right turn, S. This takes place some way above the valley with the buildings seen down below through the trees. Go S along this ancient sunken track for several minutes before turning left, E, to go down a few metres to pick up another path going S. The first building you come across is the...

5.20 Ermita de Nuestra Señora de Idoya, 825m. *16th-century chapel with attending vicarage and spring nearby.* Ignore the sign pointing left to Isaba but pass through the hermitage to find on the other side a cobbled track going S to...

5.35 Isaba, 818m. *Hotels, bars, restaurants, shops and HI hostel.*

Day 9: Isaba - Zuriza

Distance:	18.5 kilometres
Height gain:	1300 metres
Height loss:	890 metres
Time:	6hrs 30mins

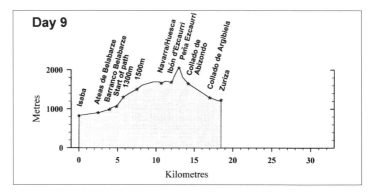

Today's stage is a superb mountain expedition in its own right, taken as a one day hike. But, as part of a continuous long distance walk, it is extremely arduous, with 300 metres of crag to surmount after hauling loads up some 1000 metres to the foot of the south face of Peña Ezcaurri. One cannot believe that walkers are expected to surmount this obstacle but the gully cannot be seen until right up against the rock as it starts diagonally left behind the first pillars. Keenness to scramble is needed here so a decision has to be made to avoid this stage by the northern route if it is too intimidating. Water will have to be carried as, after the early river, there is none.

Maps: *Editorial Alpina Ansó. The GR11 route is incorrectly marked to the summit of Peña Ezcaurri.*

Camping: *At Zuriza with bar and restaurant. The water is foul at Ibón d'Ezcaurri in high summer.*

0.00 Isaba, 818m. From the telephone boxes in the town centre on the main road, cross the bridge E and go up the Calle Barrikata to soon reach an old path passing by the small hermitage of Belén. The path joins a pista coming up from the lower part of

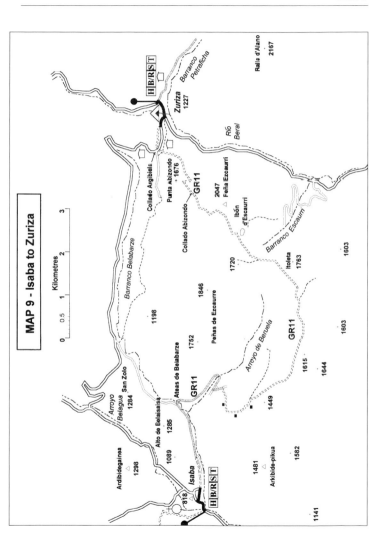

MAP 9 - Isaba to Zuriza

Kilometres

0   0.5   1   2   3

Peña Ezcaurri from Zuriza

town. Follow the pista E to the junction of the two valleys called...
0.35 Ateas de Belabarze, 920m (Sign says 920m). Turn right
across the bridge, S then SE. *If you have decided to give this part a
miss, then carry straight on, NE, to the Isaba to Zuriza road, turning E
to Zuriza or try the old GR11 route through the forest above and to the
south of the Barranco Belabarze, though I understand that the markings
are no longer present.* In just over a kilometre the pista crosses the
stream, becomes earth and begins to climb steeply NW. Go up
this for a few minutes passing an earth pista climbing very
steeply to the left. A few metres later turn sharp left, S, along
another earth pista with waymarks present and a fence above on
the right. Keep a look out on the right, for when the fence turns
sharply upward, you must leave the pista, waymarks, to find a
path beside the fence ascending WSW. When the fence makes
another sharp turn to the right, ignore old marks on posts and
continue upwards, W, on grass up to a ruined hut. Beware of
biting flies in the open grassy areas. Continue W to a wide track
and then S over grass to another ruined hut. Go SE from here on
another wide path following waymarks to a third ruined

building. Continue upwards passing to the right of some rocky outcrops. Continue SE up the ridge to reach a grassy place overlooking a valley to the northeast. There are a number of tracks ahead contouring the mountainside and some waymarks, but all arrive well below the pass beyond Itoleta. The true route continues to climb SE before gaining the top of the ridge with its grassy summits. Then it turns E to gain the SW ridge of Itoleta to contour NE, level with the pass ahead. The path passes above the treeline to reach the border between Navarra and Aragòn at the pass above the Barranco Ezcaurri...

3.15 Pass, 1740m. Continue N passing rocky outcrops on the E side, climbing slightly, avoiding a clear path that goes left around the last rise which would take you to the pass between Peñas de Ezcaurre and Peña Ezcaurri. Continue down NE to the west side of the most westerly glacial lake of the Pyrenees...

3.40 Ibón d'Ezcaurri, 1680m. *Please note that the Spanish Guide map shows the route passing to the wrong side of the lake. The only escape from here involves a long descent SE then S to the Barranco de Ezcaurri and a 5 kilometre road walk up to Zuriza. It is not possible to go through the pass on the left and find an easy and safe way down, without first climbing back to the summit plateau.* Follow the marks to the south face of the mountain. A short steep section gains access to the ascent gully. There are two more steep steps, awkward but not difficult, before coming out on the summit plateau. Follow waymarks NE to the summit platform...

5.00 Peña Ezcaurri, 2047m. Leave the summit slightly west of N to pick up the obvious marked descent route on the north flank, which takes an easy fault line down the northern slabs. This goes down to the clear pass...

5.40 Collado Abizondo, 1640m. Go down NE through the dense stunted beech wood, turning back to the mountain for a while before continuing down NE. The steepest section will be very slippery in wet conditions. The waymarks lead down to the road a few metres below the...

6.10 Collado Argibiela, 1290m. Turning one's back to Navarra, cross the road and follow the path down, E, to join the road again in about one kilometre. Follow the road to the campsite with its entrance above, on the north side...

The author beside the summit of Peña Ezcaurri

6.30 Zuriza, 1227m. *Excellent campsite, open all year, with helpful staff. Hotel, bar, restaurant, shop and dormitories with a free hut nearby, keys at the bar. Out of season, when the shop is closed, staff will bring in supplies from Ansó upon request.*

Day 10: Zuriza - Selba d'Oza

Distance:	15 kilometres
Height gain:	735 metres
Height loss:	825 metres
Time:	4hrs 40mins

They said, at the campsite, that it was a lovely walk and it proved to be so. Towering limestone crags overlook the start and no major difficulties make for a relaxing day with the certainty of a good meal in the evening.

Maps: *Editorial Alpina Ansó.*

Camping: *Selba d'Oza or La Mina. It might be a good idea to check at Zuriza that the campsite at Selba d'Oza is open, as it had closed down but now should be open again. There are many places to camp along the Barranco de Petraficha also.*

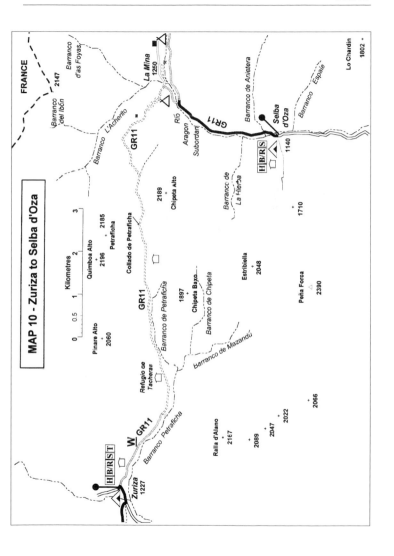

MAP 10 - Zuriza to Selba d'Oza

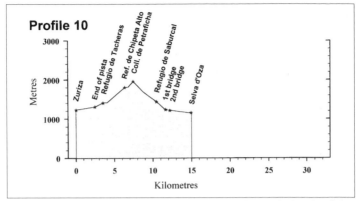

0.00 Zuriza, 1227m. Take the pista, SE, on the right bank of the Barranco Petraficha passing a new water point after 15mins. About 2.5 kilometres from Zuriza, as the pista goes across the stream, take the path steeply ascending E past the...

0.50 Refugio de Tacheras, 1410m. Continue climbing NE above the hut, eventually passing above a grassy area with a metal shepherd's hut, below to the right (the Refugio de Chipeta Alto). Continue the ascent, E, with the trail following a rocky ridge in the centre of the valley. As usual, the first pass seen is not the actual one that lays further back and up against the steep SE ridge of Petraficha. The GR11 gains height beforehand to easily reach ..

2.50 Collado de Petraficha, 1961m. Go down the obvious valley ahead, E, but look out for the waymarks leading off right from the main track just before the stream takes to a narrow ravine. About one kilometre later, look out for waymarks leading left from the main path. The trail turns SE passing the old Refugio de Saburcal and snow depth pole, seen to the left, where the track becomes indistinct on the grass. Continue SE across the grass soon finding the path again which goes down many zigzags to the open area of...

4.05 La Mina, 1230m. *This used to be the staging area for the GR11 but now one is expected to go S to Selva de Oza, returning the next day. There are plenty of places to camp.* If you are not going to Selva d'Oza, cross the bridge and take a waymarked path on the right

Refugio de Tacheras perched on the ridge

across the pastures to another bridge and access to the pista beyond. However, if you are going to the campsite, do not cross the bridge but turn right, SW, taking the pista which crosses another bridge to join the road going S. Turn right along the road and in about 2.5 kilometres you reach the clearing of...

4.40 Selba d'Oza, 1140m. *Large campsite with hotel, restaurant, bar, shop facilities and a bothy. Open April to mid-September.*

Day 11: Selba d'Oza - Candanchú

Distance:	25 kilometres
Height gain:	1080 metres
Height loss:	670 metres
Time:	6hrs 25mins

A long but pleasant day with an easy walk along the left bank of the Río Aragón Subordan before climbing steeply into the long, flat hanging valley of Aguas Tuertas. Spectacular rough mountain scenery around the Ibón d'Estanés before a short excursion into France and then back into Spain to the ski complex of Candanchú.

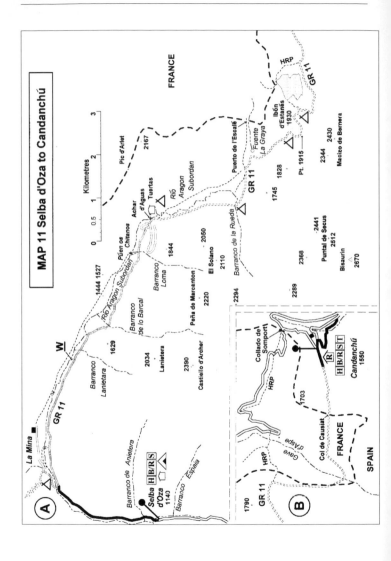

MAP 11 Selba d'Oza to Candanchú

FRANCE

HRP

GR 11

Pic d'Arlet
2167

Ibón d'Estanés
1930

Macizo de Bernera
2430
2344
Pt. 1915

Puerto de l'Escalé

Achar
d'Aguas
Tuertas

Río
Aragon
Subordan

Fuente
La Graya

GR 11

1828
1745

Barranco de la Rueda

Púen os
Chitanos

Río Aragon Subordán

El Solano
2050
2110

2441
Puntal de Secus
2512
Bisaurin
2670

2368

Barranco
de lo Barcal

Barranco
Loma
1844

Peña de Marcanton
2220

2289

2294

1444 1527

Collado del
Somport

Candanchú
1550
H|B|R|S|T
R

Barranco
Lanietera

W

1629

2034
Lanietera

Castiello d'Archer
2390

HRP

1703

Gave d'Aspe

Col de Causiat

FRANCE

SPAIN

GR 11

La Mina

GR 11

Barranco de Anietera

Selba
d'Oza
1140
H|B|R|S

Barranco España

A

HRP

1790

B

Kilometres
0 0.5 1 2 3

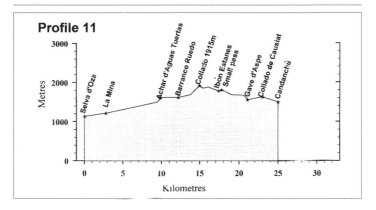

Profile 11

Maps: *Editorial Alpina Candanchú.*

Camping: *At the Achar and Barranco de la Rueda ends of the Aguas Tuertas, just before the pass at 1915m and in the small hanging valley above Ibón Estanés.*

0.00 Selba d'Oza, 1140m. Retrace steps north passing by the bridge crossed in yesterday's stage. Within a few metres the road becomes a pista which is followed as it turns E into the Guarrinza valley, which seems to be filled with all the cows of Spain during the summer and which also contains the Río Aragon Subordan. It turns ESE easily ascending the left side of the valley. About 3km from the bridge, a water point is reached, and after 7km the pista makes a long loop westwards while the GR11 climbs steeply ESE to the narrow opening to the hanging valley above called...

2.15 Achar d'Aguas Tuertas, 1620m. *Entrance to the long water meadow of Aguas Tuertas that is very wet at snow melt times. A quite delightful place.* Follow the rocky path S which leads to the flat valley and a new hut with two rooms. Follow a faint trail and waymarks, slightly east of south, always on the true right, west, of the valley, to the crossing of the Barranco de la Rueda and dry ground. *A 'sock' crossing in May!* Here, turn E towards the Puerto de l'Escalé which lies at the end of the grassy area and some 2km away. After about 10-15mins keep a look out for waymarks leading off right across grass SE from the main path. Continue

Looking south, Aguas Tuertas

SE climbing up a well-marked trail to a small pass that gains access to the Ibón Estanés valley...

4.00 Collado, 1915m. Go down NE, at first, following the marks towards and well above the western end of the lake, and at about 1800m take the right branch of the path, SSW, across a small hanging valley, turning eastwards to the SE end of the lake called...

4.50 Ibón d'Estanés, 1780m. From the end of the lake, go up E to another small pass, 1810m, going down, NE, on the other side, on the left side of the valley, to a grassy place, at about 1680m, where the HRP leaves to the left. The GR11 turns right, S, over a grassy rise, gently descending into France near to the border marker No.293 some 40m to the left. The route follows the border for a while, goes into the beech wood and turns SE to go down to cross the Gave d'Aspe at about 1560m. Traverse, with great care, a very steep earth and scree slope, caused by a landslide, and then follow the path NE and E out of the wood to the wide pass of...

6.05 Col de Causiat, 1630m. *Border again, back into Spain with the ski resort below. Signpost to Ibón Estanés.* Continue E passing between two hollows down to the road that brings you past the Alpine Military School to...

6.25 Candanchú, 1550m. *Hotels, restaurants, bars, and telephones do not seem to function during the summer. You arrive at a sharp bend in the main road through the resort. Up and left goes to the Collado de Somport and the main road into France. A couple of hundred metres up this road, on the right, is the only shop, with bar, that sells provisions during the spring and summer. Down right, E, and taking the first turning on the right, which bends to the SW, leads to the Refugio 'El Aguila' on the left, which may only open during the evening.*

Day 12: Candanchú - Sallent de Gállego

Distance:	22.3 kilometres
Height gain:	880 metres
Height loss:	1125 metres
Time:	6hrs 10mins

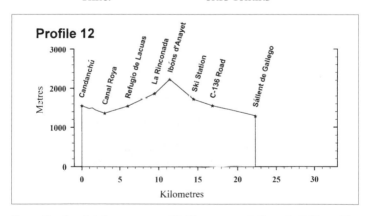

From Candanchú there are two GR 11 routes to Sallent de Gállego. The recommended one is through the Canal Roya valley and Anayet lakes and this is the one described here. It is a superb walk with plenty of opportunities to camp as required. At the head of the valley the path surprisingly surmounts a ring of steep slabs, winding along grassy

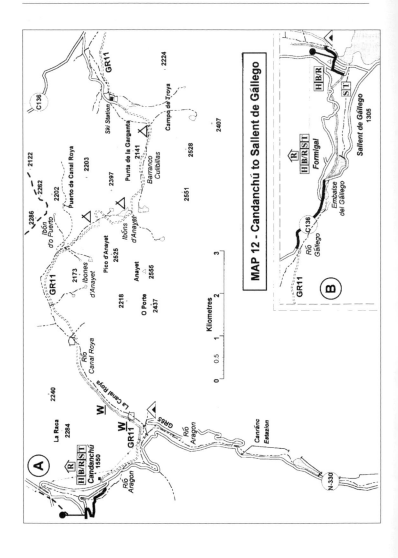

MAP 12 - Candanchú to Sallent de Gállego

fault lines to join the Anayet lakes where Pic du Midi d'Ossau towers to the north in France.

Maps: *Editorial Alpina Candanchú and Panticosa.*

Camping: *Plenty of places from above the Lacuas hut to the pista. There is also a campsite at Sallent de Gállego and another below the entrance to the Canal Roya valley. This can be reached by following the yellow GR65 variant and GR11 Canal Izas marks down to a road. Turn left, cross a bridge and Camping Canfranc will be found up and on the left.*

0.00 Candanchú, 1550m. From the refugio 'El Aguila' go down the road which turns E to join another before reaching the N-330 where there is a GR11 notice. Cross the main road taking the pista which climbs SE, starting a few metres up the road, N, which passes by a hut to reach a little pass. This is part of the Santiago de Compostella trail variant which goes down the left side of the river. The trail climbs over two earthen banks and down some steps before turning E into the Canal Roya, passing under power lines, to join the pista that comes up from the road below and shortly comes to the junction with the other GR11 route to Sallent via Collado de Izas and where the Santiago trail also turns off to the right. A few metres on is the spring and picnic area of...

0.35 Merendero de Canal Roya, 1360m. *Wild camping possible below.* Follow the pista into the Canal Roya, NE. After about 1km a water point is reached and 1km later the pista becomes a path leading to, at about 1550m, a bridge over the stream just below...

1.20 Refugio de Lacuas, 1550m. *Grubby but useable for emergencies.* Continue along the true left side of the stream crossing one from the Anayet peaks on the right. At 1800m the track is joined from the left by the path from the Coll du Portalet on the frontier via the Puerto de Canal Roya to the north. However, continue along the left side of the main stream turning SE to enter the area below the slabs called...

2.45 La Rinconada, 1870m. Follow the trail to the waymark at the start of the climb, towards the left of the slabs. In season, especially at week-ends, walkers descending the slabs will indicate the start. Otherwise it becomes apparent as one approaches the left-hand side of the lowest part of the slabs. Once

Pic du Midi d'Ossau, from Ibones D'Anayet

on the crag follow the path as it clings to the steep rocks. Later, as the route becomes less clear, surmount the last hump in a SE direction to reach the...

3.40 Ibóns d'Anayet, 2227m. An idyllic and popular spot. The mountain to the north is the Pic du Midi d'Ossau. The way down to the Barranco Culibillas is to the SE where it soon becomes apparent as the last grassy moraine is topped. *The mountains then seen in the distance framed by the crags of the valley are the Infiernos, whose pass on the left side carries the GR11 towards Panticosa.* However, to matters at hand, go down the Culibillas valley crossing the stream three times until finally keeping to its right side. The path soon joins the...

4.25 Pista, 1770m. *This now goes down to the new Formigal ski station where a road continues down to the Corral de las Mulas on the C-136 road. The new ski station has obliterated the old route. It now is much quicker to walk down the new road to the C-136 to the junction with the GR route. The GR11 is, eventually, well marked but little used now. The following instructions are for those who wish to still use the old GR11 way.* Go down this pista to the ski station and turn right across a large carpark area. At the end, turn left, NE, and contour the steep hillside ahead, at about the same height as the parking area, to locate the first waymarks on one of the tracks that cross the hillside. Follow waymarks across two boulder fields and down steep grass to a bridge over the Gallego river, thus joining the...

5.20 C-136 road, 1550m. Go down this for 1.5km, passing the road turning to Formigal and Sallent, taking a farm track to the left just before another bridge over the river. This goes down to Sallent with shortcuts crossing the road a few times before arriving at...

6.10 Sallent de Gállego, 1305m. *Hotels, restaurants, bars, shops, bank, telephone and a campsite.*

Day 13: Sallent de Gállego - Balneario de Panticosa

Distance:	24 kilometres
Height gain:	1520 metres
Height loss:	1185 metres
Time:	9hrs

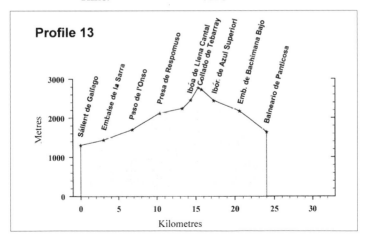

It would be a shame to walk from Sallent to Balneario de Panticosa in one day, passing so quickly through such an absolutely delightful

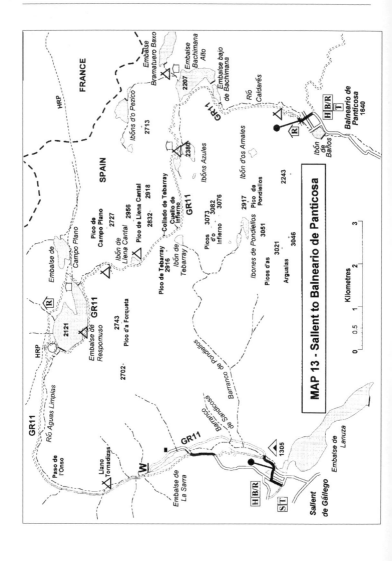

MAP 13 - Sallent to Balneario de Panticosa

mountain area. It is recommended that good weather is chosen and at least two days used for this stage. The new Refugio can be used if without a tent but those with camping kit will relish the high camps with stunning scenery. Balneario de Panticosa lies just 8.5km away to the east of Sallent, on the other side of a 3000 metre ridge. The GR11 takes a sweeping curve to the north following the Río Aguas Limpias to cross the ridge coming from the Grande Fache, 3005 metres, in the NE on the border with France. At Balneario de Panticosa there is nowhere to re-provision but a picnic lunch can be ordered at the Refugio.

Maps: *Editorial Alpina Panticosa/Formigal. The profile and map in the Spanish guide are incorrect in distance and height and the new Refugio is shown at the side of the wrong stream.*

Camping: *Llano Tornadizas, around Respomuso, below or beside Ibón de Llena Cantal, beside the Azul lakes and a small camping area above Panticosa, but too far away to use the village for meals.*

0.00 Sallent de Gállego, 1305m. *A new route has been opened, using an ancient track that climbs to the road below the Embalse de la Sarra.* Leave by NE of town, keeping to the western side of the river. Continue along the pista, ignoring a turn left after about 1 kilometre. Then after a minute or so turn left up the ancient track, recently cleared (1999) and follow to the road. Turn right and just before the dam take the track to the left just before the dam of the Sarra lake...

0.35 Embalse de La Sarra, 1438m. Follow the track on the western side of the lake, passing picnic site with water supply at the end of the lake. Continue, NNW, to follow the pista upwards. In about 1km, a grassy area beside the stream is passed, on the right. This is Llano Tornadizas, suitable for a wild camp. The trail continues north with the stream down to the right. The valley narrows at...

1.55 Paso de l'Onso, 1700m. The trail gradually turns towards the east with Llano Cheto, a grassy area, down below to the right through the trees. Continue climbing E, a seemingly never-ending trail, until quite suddenly the enormous dam of Respomuso looms high overhead. The final climb takes to the steps up to the...

3.25 Presa de Respomuso, 2121m. *The chapel is called Capella de la*

Cuella de Infierno from the small tarn called Ibón Azul Superior

Virgin de las Nieves. To visit or stay at the new Refugio, climb the zigzags above the chapel to gain a trail E, well above the lake, which goes all the way to the hut in about 20 minutes. In early June, snow may make passing the lake on its southern shore hazardous. If this is so, it may also make the crossing of the Collado de Tebarray difficult or impossible. Cross the dam, taking good care in high winds, as the wind velocity increases dramatically as it is funnelled through the gap in the centre, over which an iron walkway takes pedestrians to the other side. Follow the track around the south of the lake until it is possible to turn right, SSE, into the Llena Cantal valley that is beyond the east end of the lake. It is possible to camp in this valley or climb up the next steep section to...

5.00 Ibón de Llena Cantal, 2450m. *The massif to the NNE is that of Balaitous, the summit being 3151m.* The Collado de Tebarray lies to the SE to the left of the conical peak of Tebarray above to the south. There is usually a snow slope leading to the pass facilitating the first part of the ascent. A short, steep, broken gully is climbed to gain the narrow...

6.05 Collado de Tebarray (or Piedrafita), 2782m. *This is about as high as the GR11 gets, only surpassed during day 36.* Go down the very steep slope towards the lake to reach the track contouring SE, well above the lake, to the next pass...

6.20 Cuello de Infierno, 2721m. *From here a popular ascent of the Infiernos can be made. The first difficulty can be turned on the right by gaining another ridge further on.* Go down the valley to the east, often over snow, passing to the north of the Ibóns Azules, a popular place for a tent. Continue E to reach the large lake of...

7.30 Embalse Bachimana Alto, 2207m. Cross the stream coming from the Azul lakes and continue SE with the Bachimana lake on the left. It is important not to go down the left side of this lake. The track turns SW around the north of the lower lake before going steeply down the Caldarés valley, S, passing a small camping area before arriving at...

9.00 Balneario de Panticosa, 1640m. *Guarded hut to the right, Casa de Piedra, open all year, 120 places, bar and meals. Hotels, restaurants, bars and telephone.*

Day 14: Balneario de Panticosa - San Nicolás de Bujaruelo

Distance:	19.5 kilometres
Height gain:	940 metres
Height loss:	1240 metres
Time:	6hrs 50mins

Another day to be savoured, passing through the granite wilderness on either side of the Brazato pass. Then, the long easy walk down the Ara valley to Bujaruelo, justifiably popular during the summer for camping and picnicking. One can go farther, if desired, to another campsite some two kilometres down the pista or even all the way down to the road at Puente de los Navarros, where there is yet another campsite, and another beside the hotel, one kilometre south along the road to Torla. There is a small but comprehensive supermarket at this last site that may still sell basic mountaineering equipment. Careful planning of victualling is needed from now on. In season, during the next four stages, meals can be obtained at Bujaruelo, the campsites below and only at the Refugio de Góriz if in residence. Supplies can only be

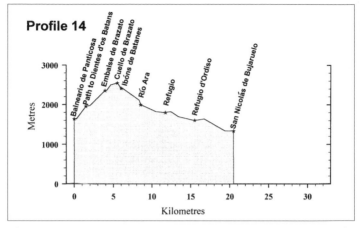

obtained with certainty at the campsite below Bujaruelo, the supermarket at the campsite below the Puente de Navarros and at Parzán.

Maps: *Editorial Alpina Panticosa/Formigal, and Valle de Ordesa.*

Camping: *Campsites as above, with wild camping possible below the Ibóns de Batanes and at the Ara/Espelunz junction. The campsite at the Bujaruelo bridge did not open for the summer until 23rd June in 1999.*

0.00 Balneario de Panticosa, 1640m. From the SE of the town, take the steps that go up SE beside the Casa Belio which go the Fuente de la Saluz, where an old path is followed shortly to take another to the NE. Then, near to an avalanche retaining wall, take a path on the right SE that climbs steeply, zigzagging through the pines to the signpost to Ibones de Labaza and Diens d'os Batans, about one hour from the town. Do not take this path but go S to climb a grassy rise to the boulder wilderness. Follow the trail round to the left to climb NE then again SE, crossing the stream coming down from the left from Ibóns Alto d'o Brazato. Continue, generally SE to reach the large dammed lake...

2.20 Embalse de Brazato, 2360m. Go round the north end of the lake, then turn N to reach the west shoulder of Pico de Racias above the upper lakes. The pass lies a few hundred metres away to the NE...

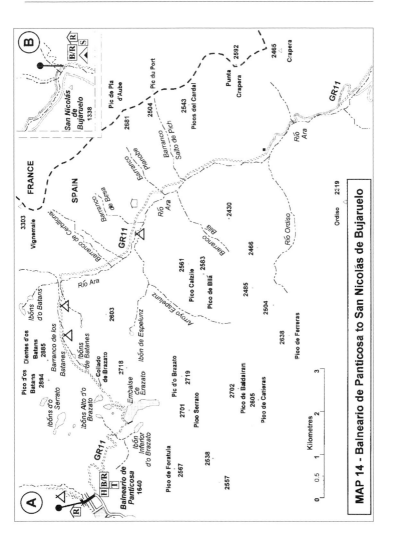

MAP 14 - Balneario de Panticosa to San Nicolás de Bujaruelo

3.00 Collado de Brazato, 2550m. *The huge massif ahead is Vignemale, containing in its 3000m horseshoe crest the large and steep Glacier d'Ossoue.* Continue NE down the valley ahead, passing a large grassy area on the right, keeping to the left of the Ibóns de Batanes. Then cross the outlet stream of the last lake to the right side, E, past more granite blocks to easier terrain, eventually to reach the...

4.10 Ara River, 2000m. Cross the river. This can be tricky when filled with melt water or after heavy rain. Above there is a clear path. Turn right and follow past a...

5.00 Hut, 1800m. *Good condition, 8 places in 2 rooms with water nearby.* Carry on down the track to...

5.50 Refugio d'Ordiso, 1580m. Dirty and not inviting. From here a pista continues down the left of the valley which is followed, always on the left of the river, all the way to...

6.50 San Nicolás de Bujaruelo, 1338m. *There is a refugio attached to the bar at Bujaruelo with full services. The campsite has a new site block with shop and excellent toilets. The path continues on the left, north, of the river but the refugio/bar/restaurant and campsite are across the medieval bridge. The refugio/bar is open from Easter to the end of October but is expensive. From here a pista goes down the right side of the river to join the path at the Santa Elena bridge. A footbridge has been built across the river Ara to access the campsite/bar restaurant situated 30mins downstream from Bujaruelo. Facilities are good here, at Camping Bujaruelo just 30 minutes from Bujaruelo bridge. There is also a path ENE to the road, in France, at the Port de Gavarnie.*

Day 15: Bujaruelo - Refugio de Góriz

Distance:	22 kilometres
Height gain:	1130 metres
Height loss:	310 metres
Time:	5hrs 45mins

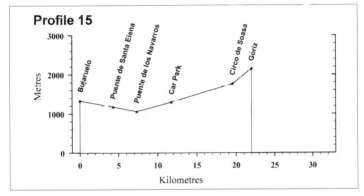

Profile 15

This stage takes us through canyon country. First, the Garganta de Bujaruelo, then the larger Ordesa canyon within the boundary of the Parque National de Ordesa y Monte Perdido. Created in 1918 and extended in 1982 this national park was the vision of one Lucien Briet, captivated by the outstanding beauty of the area, who first visited Ordesa in 1891. Waymarking ceases at the car park and starts again at the little bridge in the Circo de Soasa. Beware though, GR11 type waymarks appear all around the canyon as marked approach routes. Drink only from the side streams as the main Arazas river comes down from the Góriz hut where the Barranco de Góriz may still be used as a loo by some! A day to savour.

Maps: *Editorial Alpina Valle de Ordesa. This 1:40,000 map is recommended especially if further walks in the area are anticipated and it is preferable to the SGE ones or the Editorial Alpina Bigorre.*

Camping: *No camping allowed in the National Park with the exception of the area SE from the Góriz hut, where tents can be erected early evening but must be lowered and held down with rocks during the day. If you don't do it the guardians will!*

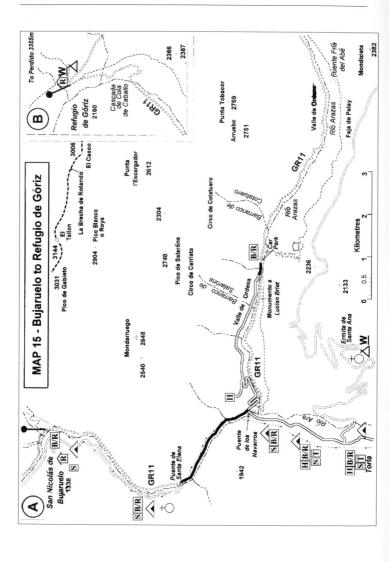

MAP 15 - Bujaruelo to Refugio de Góriz

0.00 Bujaruelo, 1338m. From the bar, go back over the bridge turning right to follow the path S along the left side of the river Ara. This wanders through woods past a path on the right, which goes to Camping Bujaruelo via a small foot-bridge, to reach the bridge, Puente de Santa Elena, where the pista crosses to the path side. Follow the pista all the way down to the road bridge of...

1.15 Puente de los Navarros, 1060m. *The National Park starts here. A new campsite lies 10mins down the road S with supermarket and bar/restaurant. A further 10mins S is the Hotel and Camping Ordesa with bar/restaurant and supermarket. In another 2km is the small town of Torla, with a mountain equipment shop in the new shopping arcade.* A new track, on the right, passes beneath the road to cross the river Arazas by a concrete bridge. Climb up the other side to reach a pista which was the old way to Ordesa before the road was built. Turn left, NE, to follow this track called 'Camino de Turieta Bajo'. *Although most of the track into and along the canyon is very wide I have marked it on the sketch map as a path rather than a pista as it only takes foot traffic (apart from any official park vehicles).* Continue along this track above the river on the true left of the valley passing the monument to Lucien Briet opposite the Puente de Ordesa, to another bridge, 'Puente de las Fuentes'. Cross over the Arazas here to the road just before the...

2.15 Ordesa car park, 1300m. *Large bar/restaurant on the left.* Go along the wide, and popular path E on the right side of the river, climbing easy slopes steepening somewhat past the cascades to the open space of the Circo de Soasa. *The large waterfall at the head of the valley is called Cascada de Cola de Caballo, the Horse Tail Falls.* Continue NE towards the falls until a small footbridge allows the crossing of the river at...

4.25 Circo de Soasa, 1760m. On the right, E, will be seen a large scree slope with a path winding up it. This is the way to easily gain the first shelf above the canyon and the way of the GR11. The adventurous, if they wish, can climb out by the iron rods, 'Las clavijas', found in the obvious cave to the right of the falls. Once above the canyon wall follow the trail upward, NW and then NNW, through slopes of English irises, in season, over easy rock steps and grassy terraces to...

5.45 Refugio de Góriz, 2160m. *Open all year, 150 places, meals*

*The north face of Vignemale. This spot can be reached by
using a pass at the head of the Ara valley*

service, water point and camping area. The climb NE from here to
Monte Perdido, third highest in the Pyrenees, is spectacular but easy.
A late start is required to allow the snow to soften. It is a long but
rewarding trip through snow filled hanging valleys with seemingly no
easy exit, but one is always found. One has nothing but admiration for
those who first worked out this way to the top. Please note that there is
good grass and water just below the Collado d'Arrablo but this is still
within the boundary of the National Park.

Day 16: Refugio de Góriz - Circo de Pineta

Distance:	13.5 kilometres	**Variant:**	11.5 kilometres
Height gain:	880 metres		590 metres
Height loss:	1750 metres		1460 metres
Time:	7hrs 10mins		6hrs 40mins

*The GR11 makes its way around the south side of Sum de Ramond via
ledges and gullies, some very narrow and dangerous in snow. It is
essential to enquire at the Góriz hut or at the Parador Hotel in the*

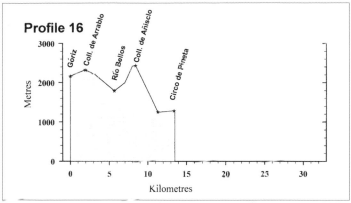

Pineta valley, if coming from that direction, to ascertain the condition of the route before setting out. It is also important to assess whether you or your party are comfortable scrambling with such exposure across the upper wall of the Añisclo canyon. There is a cable to assist in the awkward gully. Nevertheless, this is a superb route if the above conditions are met. However, as more and more walkers are taking to this mountain area, in 1989 a second easier route was waymarked into the Añisclo canyon below a water spout called the Fuén Blanca and from there climbing out to join the first route at the Añisclo pass. The original route via the high ledges is now the variant. Both routes are described here, as the Añisclo canyon route has changed from an optional extra to an essential alternative stage, and then to become the safest and officially recognised route.

Maps: *Editorial Alpina Valle de Ordesa.*

Camping: *Circo de Pineta.*

0.00 Refugio de Góriz, 2160m. Take the path SE from the hut which ascends gradually to reach...

0.30 Collado de Arrablo, 2329m. For the Anisclo canyon route, take the path SE going down, over grass, with the Barranco Arrablo to the left. Continue along the SW edge of the gorge for about 400m until cairns and waymarks lead the way over the edge and down the first crag. **NB. Care needed descending the rock steps though these are not difficult.** Go right on the wide

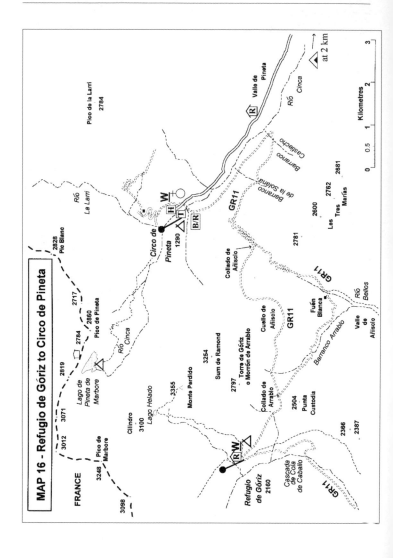

MAP 16 - Refugio de Góriz to Circo de Pineta

El Cilindro (on the way to Monte Perdido from the Góriz hut)

grassy shelf and follow the way down. Later, after another rock band, the trail crosses the stream to the left side. Steep zigzags lead down, past the Fuen Blanca seen to the left, through lush undergrowth past a cabin to...

1.45 the valley floor, 1800m. *Officially, overnight camping is permitted much lower down the canyon.* Cross the Río Vellos by a small bridge, turn left, NE, and commence the climb, on the left side of the valley. This is not difficult but seems very tiring on the steeper parts. Much higher the track crosses to the right of the stream and with many zigzags surmounts the final steep section, turning E, crossing the slope, to reach...

4.00 Collado de Añisclo, 2440m. *The first view of the descent can be quite intimidating. However the way down uses a shallow depression which removes much of the sense of exposure. Great care must be taken not to get lost on the descent. Especially do not try to reach the Parador below on a direct line, by continuing the early direction of the descent.* Go steeply down NE by zigzags over rocky ground to about 1900m where a path goes off to the left, NW, along the Faja Tormosa, signposted. **Do not take this path.** Go down E over more bands, some scrambling required, into the wood, now travelling SE. Take care to maintain the correct route as avalanche debris often crosses the trail. The Barranco Castiecho is crossed before turning NW again, passing beneath a rocky outcrop, to go along the right side of the valley to the camping area at...

7.10 Circo de Pineta, 1290m. *Hotel, telephone, camping area with small bar, GR11 notice board with map and water point behind the chapel Capella de Nuestra Senora de Pineta. Originally Romanesque and restored during the 17th century. The road goes down 13km to Bielsa to meet the road to Parzan, the Bielsa tunnel and France. If the bar is closed, drinks and meals can be had at the Parador. There is a new Refugio down the road opposite the Barranco Castiecho.*

VARIANT

0.30 Collado de Arrablo, 2329m. For the Cuello de Añisclo, turn NE along an easily ascending, wide and grassy ledge. Much later

Espelunga, on the Alano ridge, seen from the Collado Abizondo (Day 9)

Santa Barbara ridge with Peña de Aia still in view (Day 2)
Looking back to the Petraficha ridge during Day 11

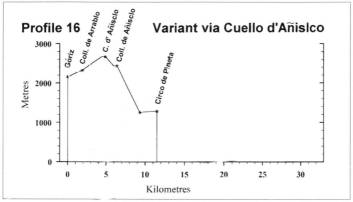

Profile 16 Góriz, Coll. de Arrablo, C. d' Añisclo, Coll. de Añisclo, Circo de Pineta **Variant via Cuello d'Añislco**

Metres — Kilometres

this becomes a narrow ledge turning N around the buttress at the end of the SE ridge of Sum de Ramond, which is called Punta d'as Olas. A little later a rocky shoot crosses the ledge. Go up this for 40m to gain another easy shelf on the right. Go along this until a boulder filled gully to the left, fitted with cable, allows access to yet another ledge, going downhill this time. Care must be taken again as this narrows. Another cable assists with safety. Continue down SE towards the Collado de Añisclo, passing to the south of a little hill that divides the pass in two, to reach...

3.30 Collado de Añisclo, 2440m. Continue as above.

Day 17: Circo de Pineta - Parzán

Distance:	18 kilometres
Height gain:	880 metres
Height loss:	1025 metres
Time:	5hrs 25mins

The highlight of this day is the view of the Perdido massif from the NE rim of the Pineta valley and the descent route of yesterday. Then the way is down the Río Real valley over rough pista then road to Parzán.

Maps: *Editorial Alpina Valle de Ordesa.*

Camping: *Apart from any camping opportunities higher up, there is no campsite at Parzán. 3km into the next day's stage beside the Barranco de Urdiceto, opposite the Barranco Fallarata, there are a number of level*

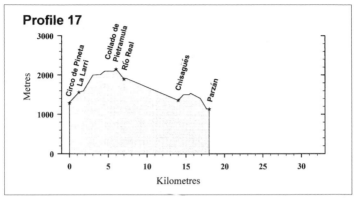

fields but care must be taken not to damage any meadow crop that might be growing.

0.00 Circo de Pineta, 1290m. Take the path going up N through the wood, which starts behind the chapel beside the water point. Be careful to find the diagonally ascending path, do not follow the one that goes straight up. Cross loops of the pista, coming from La Larri and curving around the head of the Pineta valley, to reach the flat area of...

0.45 La Larri, 1560m. Just after the farm hut, take the track going NE. Do not follow a waymark into the streambed but cross a little higher, to almost reach the Barranco Opacas. Here the trail turns SE to climb through a few zigzags to reach easier ground. Stunning views! Continue SE, with scant marking, below a hut seen high to the left, to reach a distinct flat grassy area bordered by small crags. *Camping possible here.* Cross this depression SE and in about 12 to 15 minutes climb E to the...

3.10 Collado de Pietramula, 2150m. Go down, N then NE, then down zigzags, through large boulders and ENE to cross the Río Real. Go up the left bank to gain the very rough pista and follow it down the left of the valley, SE then NE, to the road past the village of...

4.55 Chisagüés, 1360m. Continue along the road, then down many zigzags, turning right, then right again into...

5.25 Parzán, 1144m. *On the main road from Bielsa, some 3km to the*

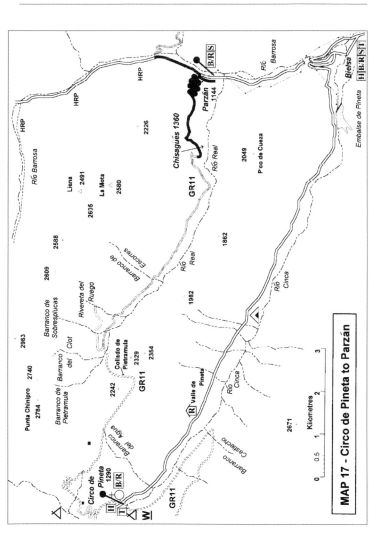

MAP 17 - Circo de Pineta to Parzán

*south, which continues north to go through the Bielsa tunnel to France.
Bar/restaurant and small supermarket beside service station. Possibility
of lodgings, ask at bar or service station.*

Day 18: Parzán - Viadós

Distance:	19.5 kilometres
Height gain:	1445 metres
Height loss:	850 metres
Time:	6hrs

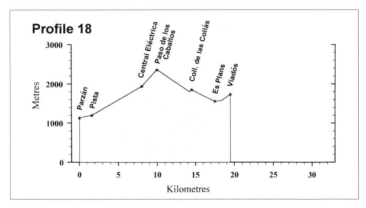

*A pleasant day, mostly pista at first, passing through a gorge along the
Barranco de Urdiceto. Then the wide grassy pass of Los Caballos below
the large dammed lake of Urdiceto. The trail down to farmland,
dominated on the right by Punta Suelza, rises three times before picking
up a pista again down to the large open area of Es Plans beside the
Cinqueta river. Supplies will be needed until the campsite shop in the
Esera valley is reached.*

Maps: *Editorial Alpina Bachimala.*

Camping: *Possibility at Campo Xusto. Beside the two smaller lakes
above the Cabullos pass to the south or at the far end of Es Plans and
above the unmanned refugio, but only open from 1st July to 21st
August. It no longer is possible to pitch a tent near to the Viadós hut.*

0.00 Parzán, 1144m. Leave the village by the main road going

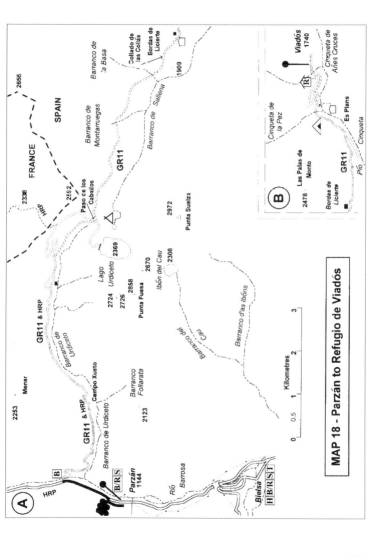

MAP 18 - Parzán to Refugio de Viadós

north passing by the GR11 notice board at the turning to Chisagüés and in about 1.5km turn right at the sign to Ordiceto. *Here a variant of the High Level Route joins from the north.* A small bar here is open in season. Follow the pista upwards along the right side of the Ordiceto or Pardina stream, first SE, then E, then NE and E again. A short cut across one of the bends in the pista can be taken just before...

2.15 Central Eléctrica de Urdiceto, 1940m. Continue along the pista for about 1.2km, until it starts to zigzag steeply, where a track is taken to the right, SE, which climbs nearer to the valley floor to...

3.20 Paso de los Caballos, 2326m. The trail can be seen ahead, SE, crossing a ridge coming down from the north. The pista continues SW to the lake. Follow the track E, at first, then SE to cross the ridge. Go down E to a grassy level where the track turns left, N then NE, to pass a small cabin. Go down the right side of the Barranco de Montarruegos (or Mantarruegas), then cross to the left bank. Continue SE through a small wood to the meadows of Sallena and a rough hut. Go SE through pines to a wide path, crossing the Barranco de la Basa. Climb SSE then ESE to the...

4.45 Collado de las Collás, 1851m. Go down the lower ground, E then SE, passing a hut on the right, now open and suitable for an overnight stop, to pick up a stony path going down to the pista. The area of farm buildings around the pista is known as Bordas de Licierte. Turn left, E, along the pista that goes down to join another larger one coming from the right, up the Cinqueta valley. Follow this NNE to the large flat grassy area of...

5.20 Es Plans, 1550m. *No longer a camping area. There is a hut with 20 places, further up. Just beyond the hut is the new campsite, only open for 6 weeks in the summer.* Continue to Viadós by crossing the Rio Cinqueta de la Pez, E, just after the junction with the Añes Cruces branch. Follow the pista until a path on the left, near a building, allows access to a short cut climbing E and crossing the pista twice before reaching...

6.00 Refugio de Viadós, 1740m. *The owners, Señor Cazarra and his wife, are very helpful. Meals and drinks, with a capacity of about 40 places. Open weekends after Easter, and 15th June to 25th of September.*

Day 19: Viadós - Refugio d'Estós

Distance:	11.5 kilometres
Height gain:	860 metres
Height loss:	710 metres
Time:	4hrs 15mins

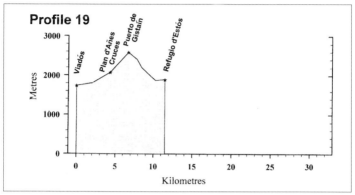

This is a short day in order to savour the lovely valleys of Añes Cruces and Estós. It can easily be extended to reach the campsites at Puente de Sant Jaime if desired. Once the Puerto de Gistaín is reached, the massif of the Maladeta can be seen to the east. This contains the highest summit in the Pyrenees, Pico de Aneto at 3404 metres. The Pico de Posets lies south from the pass but is not attainable from here. The Barranco d'Estós would have to be followed upwards to the Collado de La Paúl. The position of the Estós hut cannot be seen from the pass as it is around the right bend in the valley and over the wooded ridge seen just before the two white buildings low in the valley, but can just be identified from the right hand side of the pass.

Maps: *Editorial Alpina Posets.*

Camping: *Plan d'Añes Cruces. No camping below Estós hut nowadays.*

0.00 Viadós, 1740m. From the hut, take the wide track E through the farm buildings. *The official path, above and to the left, becomes overgrown and ends at a small landslide.* The pista becomes a path easily ascending NE along the west (right) side of the valley of

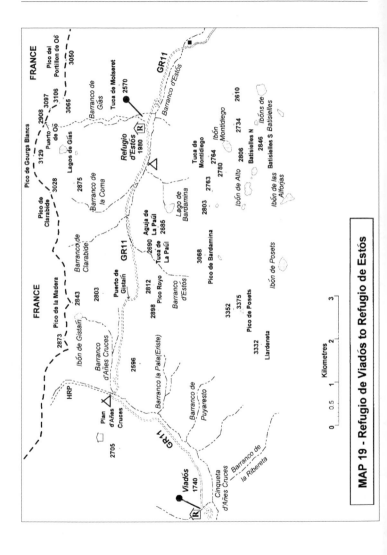

MAP 19 - Refugio de Viadós to Refugio de Estós

the Cinqueta d'Añes Cruces. A short steep ascent to the left avoids a difficult section by a stream before reaching a junction of streams...

1.10   Plan d'Añes Cruces, 2080m. Go up the obvious path climbing steeply E on the true left of the stream. This eases, eventually, to climb more gently to...

2.35   Puerto de Gistaín, 2592m. *The French border lies a short distance away to the north along the ridge to Pico de la Madera. Beside the trail to the south lies a curiosity, a stone tube filled with quartz.* Go across the pass, S, past the curiosity, following traces of a path. Go down over scree in a wide channel on the right of the valley. Usually this means making a descending traverse of the steep snow slope to reach easier ground and the Barranco d'Estós which is crossed for a while before gaining the left bank at the Barranco de Clarabide junction. Keep to the higher trail if the Refugio d'Estós is the target.

4.15 Refugio d'Estós, 1890m. *Open all year. Excellent bar and meals service. About 200 places in two tier dormitories. Self-catering kitchen. Very popular as it can be reached from a car park just above the Puente de Sant Jaime. It is mainly supplied by horseback from the end of the pista at Cabana del Turmo.*

Day 20: Estós - Refugio del Puente de Coronas

Distance:	18.5 kilometres
Height gain:	740 metres
Height loss:	650 metres
Time:	5hrs 10mins

A delightful stroll down the Estós valley and then into the narrow entrance to the Vallibierna which climbs to the south of the Maladeta massif with the highest mountain of the Pyrenees, Pico de Aneto at 3404 metres, above the head of the valley. Most of the traffic to the summit is from the north so any ascent from the south would be especially rewarding. **NB!** *There is no certainty of provisions after the campsites at Puente de Sant Jaime until reaching Espot. Meals may be had at the Hospital de Viella, which has been refurbished and is now known as Refugi de Sant Nicalau, or at the Restanca, Colomers and Amitges huts, but no guarantees of bread or other essentials. This means that sufficient*

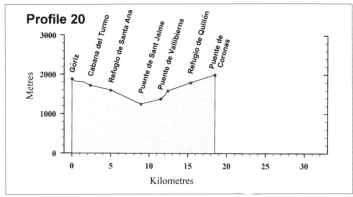

Profile 20

food for four and a half days will need to be acquired and carried. It is possible to return to France from Puente de Sant Jaime via the Puerto de Benasque to Luchon by continuing along the pista, from the Vallibierna turnoff. Then up the road to the Baños de Benasque and then a path from the car park to Hospital de Benasque thus avoiding a

The Maladeta range beyond the Estós valley

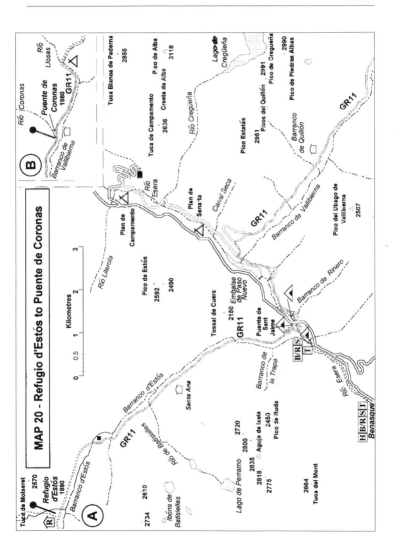

MAP 20 - Refugio d'Estós to Puente de Coronas

Kilometres
0   0.5   1   2   3

Tuca de Molseret
2570

Refugio
d'Estós
1890

R

Barranco d'Estós

GR11

Río de Batisielles

Ibóns de
Batisielles

2734   2610

Lago de Perramo   2800   2720

2835

2818   2450
2775   Aguja de Ixeia
Pico de Ruda

2664
Tuca del Mont

A

Santa Ana

Barranco d'Estós

Barranco de
la Trapa

Tossal de Cuera
2150

Pico de Estós
2592   2490

GR11

Puente de
Sant
Jaime

Embalse
de Paso
Nuevo

B/R/S
T

Río Esera

H/B/R/S/T
Benasque

Río Literola

Plan de
Campamento

Río
Esera

Plan de
Senarta

Canal Seca

GR11

Barranco de Rinero

Barranco de Valliberna

Pico del Ubago de
Valliberna
2507

B

Río Coronas

Puente de
Coronas
1980

Barranco de
Valliberna

GR11

Río
Llosas

Río
Llosas

Tuca Blanca de Paderna
2855

Tuca de Campamento
2636   Cresta de Alba

P co de Alba
3118

Río Cregueña

Lago de
Cregueña

Pico Estatis
2951   Picos del Quillón   2991

Pico de Cregueña
2990

Pico de Piedras Albas

Barranco
de Quillón

GR11

*long road walk. I understand that there is an infrequent bus service
from Camping Aneto to the valley head which would save about 3-4
hours of walking. Walking the whole distance would take about 9-10
hours without stops. There is a hut on the French side of the pass which
has meals service in season and camping is allowed by the lakes.*

Maps: *Editorial Alpina Posets, and Maladeta.*

Camping: *It is possible to camp, overnight only, below the Batisielles
stream. Camping Aneto, Chuise, or Ixeia at Puente de Jaime. Plan de
Senarta.*

0.00 Refugio d'Estós, 1890m. Go down eastwards along the left
of the valley by an obvious path, avoiding a track to the left as
the main route zigzags down. The route crosses the river by a
bridge just before the start of the pista at the Cabana del Turmo
where the Estós guides pick up supplies. Continue down the
pista on the right of the valley past the new Santa Ana cabin, 10-
15 places. Later, the pista crosses to the right again and goes
down more steeply to the steps above the car park. The steps and
then pista will lead to the road below. However, the GR11 goes
down the path ahead. This is now overgrown, so continue down
the pista zigzags taking a pista on the right, just before the road,
which leads into the Camping Aneto grounds at…

1.50 Puente de Sant Jaime, 1250m. *There are three campsites here.
One, Chuise, on the west of the main road, Ixeia, north of the bridge,
Aneto, south of the bridge. The latter with a small supermarket and
bar/restaurant. Benasque, with all services and mountain equipment
shop, is some 3 kilometres to the south via an old waymarked trail, on
the west of the road, from Camping Aneto.* A pista leaves Camping
Aneto to the north, going under the bridge. This joins with the
pista starting on the eastern side of the bridge. Follow the pista
up the left of the Río Esera, NNE, and when this starts to zigzag,
beside the dam of Paso Nuevo, take the path, E, that climbs
through the wood and a field to reach the pista again. Continue
N along the pista, crossing the…

2.50 Puente de Vallibierna, 1369m. Continue along the pista to
where the GR11 turns right, SE, at a signpost. *A short distance
ahead, N, is the camping area, with bar, of Plan de Senate. Very busy in
the holiday season.* Turn SE and climb the pista into the Vallibierna

*A street in the pleasant town of Benasque, a few kilometres
south of Puenta de Sant Jaime*

valley. The pista bears round to the left and after about 300 metres keep a look out on the right for a clear, waymarked, steep track that will short cut a long loop of the pista. Go up this, SE, and join the pista again in about 15-20 minutes. Turn right, SSE, along the pista, passing the...

4.10 Refugio de Quillón, 1790m. *Small hut of 6 places*. Continue SE along the pista to the...

5.10 Puente de Coronas, 1980m. *Just after the bridge is a hut with about 14 places. No camping allowed here anymore. It also is very busy over weekends, when a stay should be avoided. Northeast from here an ascent to the Collado de Coronas and Aneto can be made.*

The 'team' at the Puerto de Benasque on the French-Spanish border.
The GR11 can easily be reached from here

Day 21: Puente de Coronas - Hospital de Viella

Distance:	19.5 kilometres
Height gain:	1070 metres
Height loss:	1420 metres
Time:	7hrs 45mins

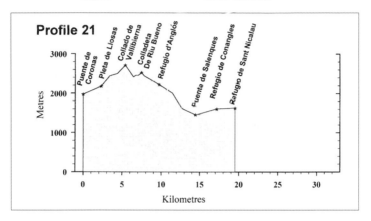

Wild and rough country ahead bejewelled with glistening glacial lakes and pools. Once over the Collado (Colladeto) de Riu Bueno the trail wanders down past lakes, passing the Refugio d'Anglós and then steeply down through a beech wood into the remote Salenques valley, where a way has been cut through debris from a huge avalanche. Low cloud could make route finding difficult. The Hospital de Viella has been renovated and now is known as Refugi Sant Nicolau. Full Refugio services are available for most of the year. One can camp and still use the meals service.

Maps: *Editorial Alpina Maladeta, and La Ribagorca.*

Camping: *Beside the two Vallivierna lakes. Beside Ibón Cap de Llauset, or above Refugio d'Anglós. Camping zone near to the Conangles hut and in the Conangles valley...*

0.00 Puente de Coronas, 1980m. Go ESE along the pista to the junction with the Barranco de Llosas where it turns NE along the right bank becoming rough and stony. Cross the stream at the

111

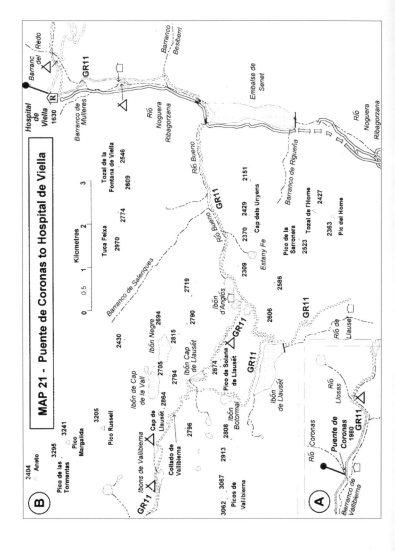

grassy area of Pleta de Llosás to climb the right of stream, with waymarked track, to...

1.30 Ibón Inferior de Vallibierna, 2440m. Go E round the north of the lake turning S to cross the entry stream (dry). Go up the rocky ledges ahead, ESE, passing to the S of the high spot. Continue E climbing down a steep section, not difficult, to a rocky depression and the SE end of the Ibón Superior. Care is needed here to select the correct line. Slightly north of east goes to the Collado dels Bocados which is to the north of Cap de Llausét and into the head of the Salenques valley. The GR11 climbs E then ESE to the south of Cap de Llausét which lies ESE from the upper lake. Go up by large boulders and snow to...

2.50 Collado de Vallibierna, 2710m. Go down E at first to a rocky combe, probably snow filled, then SE through rocky terraces and finally grass ledges to a stream at the...

3.25 GR11 Junction, 2410m. *Contouring an obvious line to the left from just above the stream can save a little effort. The right branch goes S to Ibón de Llausét and then NE to Refugio d'Anglós, or continues from the Llausét lake SE to the Refugio de Llausét and on to the small village of Aneto.* Turn left, NE, up the right of the stream, crossing it near the top, to reach the NW end of the Ibón de Cap de Llauset. Go S along the west of the lake turning E past its southern end. Then, climb SE, to the...

3.55 Colladeta de Riu Bueno, 2525m. Go down, SE, passing the first two small lakes, the Ibonets de la Cap d'Anglós, on their right side. The third lake is passed on its left side and then a fourth on the right side and then down through grass to the Ibones d'Anglós passing between lake Obago to the SW and lake del Mig to the NE. Cross the connecting stream to join the path coming from the Collado d'Anglós. Follow the waymarks that lead towards the NE with the hut seen a short distance to the left at the WSW end of the Ibón Gran d'Anglós...

4.45 Refugio d'Anglós, 2220m. *A shepherds hut, often locked.* Go round the right side of the lake and descend on the right of the stream, E, going through a small section of pine trees before turning NE to drop steeply down and through a beech wood to the Barranc de les Salenques. Pass through the avalanche debris

*The Estany de Ruis, at 2366m, is perched high and between
the Conangles and Arties valleys*

and continue along the right of the Salenques stream. The last part can be overgrown with vegetation. The metal bridge below the main road, the N-230, was found to have had been washed away in 1999 so that a crossing of the river could not be made. Climb to the right of the road bridge in the Noguera Ribagorzana valley called...

6.25 Puente de Salenques, 1460m. *Border between Aragon and Cataluna.* In order to keep off the main road as much as possible, the old route used to cross the road, E, and in about 70 metres go down right to pick up the remains of the old road coming from the Embalse de Senet. However, it is possible to cross the crash barrier and walk along beside it for most of the way to the hut some 200m ahead, GR11 notice board and parking area. Go past the hut along the carpark access road in order to cross the Ribagorzana river by a concrete bridge on the right. On the other side go left up the pista, N, now waymarked. This pista soon drops down towards the river again. On the right, marks lead up through the trees to follow a wide grassy trail which turns down to the river, following it N along its left bank. At the Barranco de Besiberri turn right to a small footbridge, a short way up E, that allows a crossing. Go down across rough pastures on the other side, NW then N, to pick up a pista going N. Pass a branch going to the camping area to the left across the river and the large Conangles hut. The pista continues, N, above the hut. Avoid the turning left to the Barcelona University Refugio. The pista becomes grassy as it winds towards the mouth of the Viella tunnel. Just as it reaches the road, take a wide grassy track, with the tunnel mouth on the left, which climbs a short way to the...

7.45 Hospital de Viella, 1630m. *Full Refugio services at Refugi Sant Nicolau.*

Day 22: Hospital de Viella - Refugio de la Restanca

Distance:	10.5 kilometres
Height gain:	770 metres
Height loss:	390 metres
Time:	4hrs 10mins

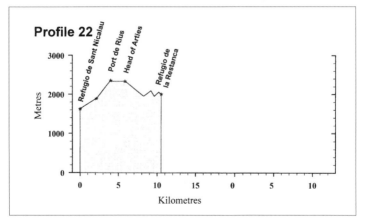

An easier day, through the Conangles valley up the delightful gully with cascading water to gain the final zigzags to Port de Rius. A popular family trip in the summer with vehicle access so near. We continue by boulder edged lakes to the head of the Arties valley at the

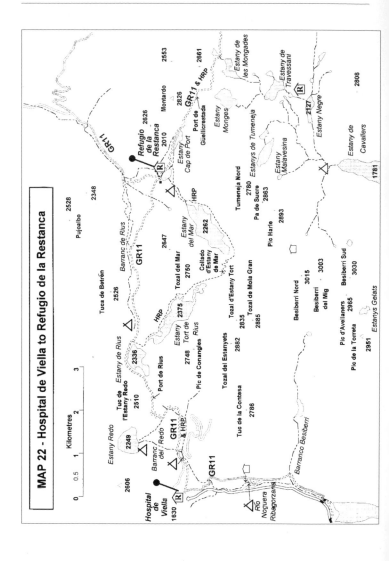

MAP 22 - Hospital de Viella to Refugio de la Restanca

Kilometres
0   0.5   1   2   3

Hospital de Viella 1630

Estany Redo
2606

Estany Redo

Tuc de l'Estany Redo 2510

Barranc del Redo

GR11 & HRP

GR11

2249

Estany de Rius 2336

Port de Rius

Pic de Conangles

Tozal dels Estanyets

Tuc de la Contesa 2786

Río Noguera Ribagorzana

Barranco Besiberri

Pic de la Torreta 2951

Pic d'Avellaners 2965

Estanys Gelats

Besiberri del Mig 3030

Besiberri Sud 3003

Besiberri 3015

Besiberri Nord

Estany de Rius

Barranc de Rius

Pujoalbo 2528

Tuca de Betrén 2526

2348

GR11

HRP

Estany Tort de Rius 2748

2647

Tozal del Mar 2750

2375

Tozal d'Estany Tort 2882

2835

Tozal de Mola Gran 2885

Estany del Mar 2262

Collado d'Estany de Mar

HRP

Refugio de la Restanca 2010

Estany Cap de Port

Port de Güellicrestada 2826

Estany Monges

Estanys de Tumeneja

Tumeneja Nord 2780

Pa de Sucre 2863

Pic Harle 2893

Estany Malavesina

Montardo 2826

2626

2553

GR11 & HRP

2661

Estany de les Mongades

Estany de Travessani R

2127

Estany Negre

Estany de Cavallers

2808

1781

eastern end of Estany de Rius, often only partly filled with its blue copper sulphate looking water. Fresh water can be had, however, a few hundred metres down the track at a small water pipe on the right. Then, easily down the Arties valley with one short steep wooded ridge to surmount to the hut.

Maps: *Editorial Alpina Ribagorca, and Val d'Aran. IGN Carte de randonnées Couserans.*

Camping: *There are camping possibilities in the lower part of the Conangles valley and also in the valley to the west, the Mulleres valley. There is also a place by Estany Redó, just off the route. Also, just below the water pipe in the Arties valley and then many places below.*

0.00 Hospital de Viella, 1630m. *The High Level Route joins from the west.* Take the track E between meadows above the Barranco de Hospital down on the right. This leads to a rocky pista which is followed for about 300m until a grassy track can be taken to the left, just before the pista goes down to cross the stream. The track goes E, crosses the Barranc del Redó (Barranco de la Escaleta) and continues through trees then rough grazing with many boulders. It climbs NE to gain a gully, not easily seen from below, with a distinct path climbing N on its left side. Near the top the path crosses to its right side and then it is necessary to watch for an ascending path to the right. Straight on goes to Estany Redó, popular with fishermen. Take the path to the right which climbs steeply NE to the narrow pass of...

1.45 Port de Rius, 2355m. *Tuc de l'Estany Redó lies to the NNW and Pic de Conangles to the SE.* Continue NE with a small lake to the right and then pass Estany de Rius by its north shore to reach at the eastern end...

2.15 Head of Arties valley (Barranco de Rius), 2340m. *The HRP goes south by the Estany Tort de Rius and Estany del Mar, a highly recommended alternative route to La Restanca.* Go down ESE along the right of the valley. The stream bed to the left is usually dry at first. In about 400m the small water point is found coming from the rock to the right of the path. A little lower, the first camping spot presents itself with water only suitable for washing. Drinking water must be collected from the pipe above. Continue down the right of the valley for another 2km or so, until a stony path to the right ESE can be taken. This climbs up and down along the side of the valley, over a small ridge, turning into a side valley SE, crosses a stream and then climbs very steeply through trees to a boggy place before going down past the old hut and so on to the dam and the new...

4.10 Refugio de la Restanca, 2010m. *About 80 places. Food and drinks service in the summer.*

Day 23: Ref. de la Restanca - Ref. de Colomers

Distance:	7.5 kilometres
Height gain:	660 metres
Height loss:	555 metres
Time:	3hrs 40mins

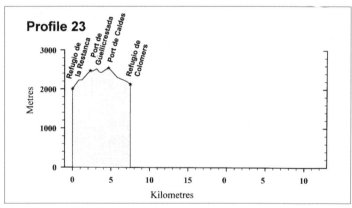

Another shortish day with plenty of time to enjoy the scenery. The walk down from the Port de Caldes is easy but the rest is rugged and quite hard. To describe the next two days as passing through the Spanish Pyrenean equivalent of the Lake District would not be amiss. A glance at the map will show seemingly countless lakes and tarns begging to be explored. Most of the summits rising from this watery landscape are quite accessible to walkers and there are places to camp almost at will. There are two routes to the Colomers hut. One goes NE down the Arties valley to turn SE to gain the Coll de Ribereta and then the hut. It is long and mostly over pista. The shorter and more delectable is described here.

Looking back to the Estany de la Restanca

Maps: *Editorial Alpina Montardo. IGN Carte de randonnées Couserans.*

Camping: *There is a grassy shelf above the Restanca to the SW towards Estany de Mar. There are possibilities from the Port de Güellicrestada onwards, though this now is the boundary of the National Park. If a visit to the Colomers hut is not required, then it is possible to contour, with some small ascents, ESE from Estany Mort to Estany Obago with many lovely spots en route, though this is not quicker.*

0.00 Refugio de la Restanca, 2010m. From the Refugio go SE steeply up the right bank of the stream to pass the Estany Cap de Port on the right. From the far end climb very steeply to the south shoulder of Montardo d'Aran and the...

1.30 Port de Güellicrestada, 2475m. National Park boundary sign. Go down E slightly, to cross a stream coming from the south side of Montardo. *Here a trail rises N, without difficulty, to the summit. Estany Monges can be seen below to the right. A path S leads to the Refugio Ventosa i Calvell below the Agullas de Travessani.* Continue ESE to an obvious small pass ahead on a SW branch off

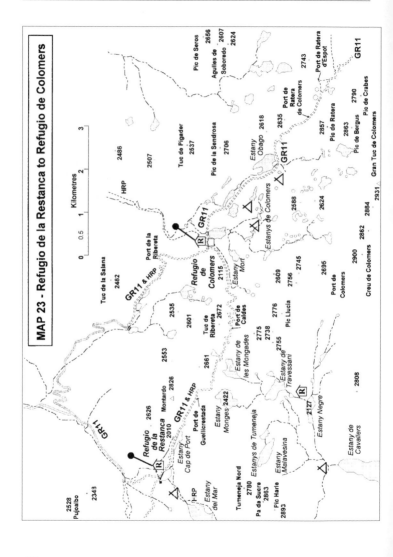

MAP 23 - Refugio de la Restanca to Refugio de Colomers

the SE ridge from the summit, following the left bank of the small stream issuing from it. *From this small pass can be seen, the Port de Caldes towards the east, the Estanys of the same name below to the left and to the right the large lake of Mengades.* Go down steeply to pass between the two upper lakes and then climb ESE to join the another path, coming up from the Ventosa hut, which is followed E to the...

2.30 Port de Caldes, 2570m. Go E past the small Cap de Rencules lake to the left and then go down to the valley E by large zigzags. Follow the path down the left of the stream to a small level grassy area where the other route joins from the left. Continue a short distance NE to...

3.40 Refugio de Colomers, 2115m. *Meals service in the season, some 30 places. When closed, the bothy, Colomers 1, is open some 50m to the SSW.*

Day 24: Refugio de Colomers - Espot

Distance:	19.5 kilometres
Height gain:	500 metres
Height loss:	1295 metres
Time:	6hrs

Profile 24

Back to longer distance walking. Today we climb to the passes of Port de Ratera de Colomers and Port de Ratera d'Espot, through delightful

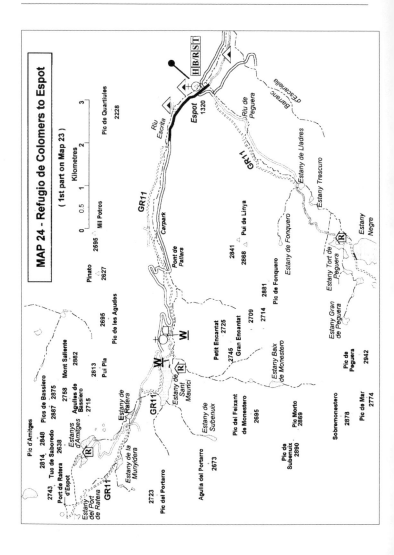

MAP 24 - Refugio de Colomers to Espot

(1st part on Map 23)

rugged mountain scenery and many lakes of the National Park of Aigüestortes and Sant Maurici. Descending through the Ratera valley, not much used now as most of the traffic goes via the Amitges refuge. Past the lower Ratera lake through the woods to the lake of Sant Maurici and along it's shores before the equally delightful walk down to Espot with even the short road sections not detracting from the sylvan experience. **There are major changes afoot on the Espot side of the National Park. The old car parking area at the eastern end of Lago Sant Maurici has been bulldozed and landscaped in the Spring of 1995. No private vehicles are now allowed to the lake, restricted access has been in force for a while. A new parking area and barrier, near to the Park boundary some four kilometres down the valley, has been constructed. The idea is that vehicle access only will be permitted to this point. However, local Landrover taxis will transport people to the lake but only all the way from Espot. The first road section has now been avoided by a newly engineered footpath to the right.**

Maps: *Editorial Alpina Montardo, and San Maurici. IGN Carte de randonnées Couserans.*

Camping: *Wild camping is not allowed now. An overnight stop would only be possible west of Estany Obago and its environs. Then the campsites at Espot would be the next location.*

0.00 Refugio de Colomers, 2115m. From the refuge cross the dam and go down to the left by some rail tracks to pick up the path going E up to a small pass turning SE to go down to Estany Long (Llarg) passing its SW side. Continue SE along the SW side of the small Estany Redó and the stream to...

0.50 Estany Obago, 2236m. This is also passed on its southwest side. Turning left round the head of the lake the route crosses a stream and climbs E, then SE, with the mass of Pic de Ratera to the right, to reach the....

1.50 Port de Ratera de Colomers, 2580m. Continue across the pass, SE then ESE, past a small pool on the left, to reach...

2.00 Port de Ratera d'Espot, 2534m. *Please note that the IGN 1:50,000 map wrongly shows the route of the GR11 here. In the summer the Ratera valley will be most appreciated as it avoids the dust and Landrovers plying trade to the Amitges refuge. Remember, while in the*

Lago de Sant Maurici

National Park waymarking will only consist of the occasional painted post or National Park footpath sign (metal post with silhouette walker on attached plaque). Go down SE passing above and to the left of the Estany del Port de Ratera. The path climbing straight ahead E goes to the Amitges refuge but be careful to find the track going down into the Ratera valley S to SE with occasional post markers. The path goes down the left side of the stream, passing to the left of the Estany de la Munyidera, eventually into pines and comes out onto a pista. It is important here to be certain where on this pista you have arrived. If on the last part of the track you maintained the left side, 40m down the pista to the right is a signpost. If however you find yourself across the stream it will be necessary to turn left on the pista to find the signpost at a Y junction of pistas. *If it isn't clear, **go down**, as both branches going westwards go uphill.* Go down the pista ESE to...

3.10 Estany de Ratera, 2130m. Follow the pista down, SE, until a short distance after it has crossed the stream, the Río Ratera, look out for a track going off right, SW, with a pole marker a short

Los Encantados (Els Encantats, in Catalan), the Enchanted Ones

distance away. Take this trail which passes the Cascade below by zigzags and then down to the Sant Maurici lake where it turns along the north shore to the end by the dam of...

4.00 Estany de Sant Maurici, 1920m. *Spring and information boards on the left, obelisk on right. The pista on the right goes down to the Refugio Ernest Mallafré, 36 places, not always open outside of the holidays.* Turn slightly right, S, to follow the signposted pista going down E for about 70m and take the left branch down past a couple of small zigzags with short cuts to...

4.10 Capella de Sant Maurici, 1900m. *This is situated beyond and immediately below the old car park, not as on maps. There is a clean usable bothy on the side of the chapel with dual water spouts below. Excellent place for a lunch break or overnight stop.* Continue down the pista which shortly joins the road. A new, excellent path has been engineered just to the right. Follow this to cross the road just above the bridge called Pont de Pallars. Cross the road and continue along the path until it turns down to the right. Go straight on and up to join a grassy pista with GR11 marks on telegraph pole. Do not take the pista ascending to the left and in 2 or 3 minutes you arrive at the National Park green boundary fence and gate with GR11 post marker. Follow the main track beyond the gate with occasional and comforting GR paint marks which eventually turns right down through old dry stone walls to the Pont de Suar wooden plank bridge over the stream leading to a pista climbing up to the road once more. *The old route through the fields is no longer in use.* Go down the road for one kilometre, passing Camping Vorla. A few minutes later you arrive at...

6.00 Espot, 1321m. *The GR11 access trail from Pont de Suert, via the Colomina hut, arrives at Espot from the south-west along the Peguera valley. Hotels, restaurants, bars, two shops for provisions and two campsites below the village. For lodgings see Jaume Vidal who runs the Bar Jouquim across the bridge. There is a very small campsite just below the road barrier across the bridge on the left and just before the village. For the nearest campsite below the village do not turn left across the bridge but go straight on between the buildings down a pista, over the Peguera stream, where a back entrance can be found on the GR11 route to the site at the end of a small grassy meadow, vehicle tracks indicating the way, just under ten minutes from the village.*

Day 25: Espot - Estaon

Distance:	20 kilometres
Height gain:	1500 metres
Height loss:	1580 metres
Time:	7hr 30mins

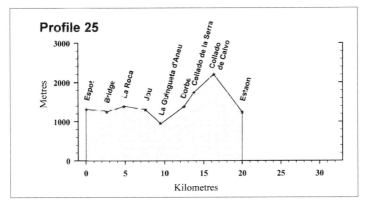

A day to be savoured. A hard day, especially in hot weather, with great variety, best started feeling fresh and in good weather. It might be a good idea to divide it into two by staying at La Guingueta if the work load seems intimidating, though it might be very hot in the valley on a summer's day. The once deserted pista to Jou has now been covered by tar-macadam and could be busy with day-trippers in the summer, but during the spring it still is a pleasant walk. The route is well marked with the exception of the section to the ridge above Dorbé. Please note that the Editorial Alpina map shows a pista from Jou to La Guingueta but this is not so. Also, IGN 1:50,000 does not show the correct route of the GR11.

Maps: *Editorial Alpina Sant Maurici, Pico d'Estats, and IGN Carte de randonnées Couserans.*

Camping: *Two campsites at La Guingueta. Wild camping only possible beyond Estaon.*

0.00 Espot, 1320m. From Espot keep to the right bank of the river Escrita passing through the buildings to follow the pista down

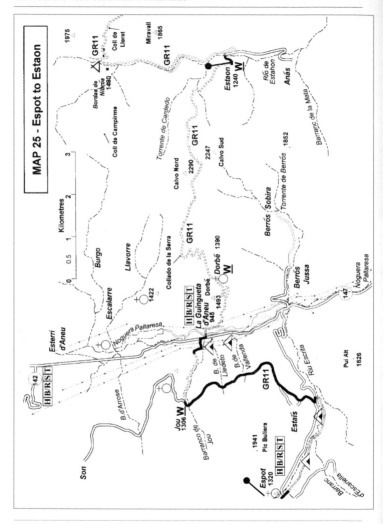

El Cilindro (on the way to Monte Perdido from the Góriz hut).
A popular exursion after Day 15

The ancient bridge at Bujaruelo (Day 14)
Overlooking the Ordesa canyon to the Circo de Cotatuero (Day 15)

past the two camp sites. Turn left down a steep pista, past the last site, crossing the Escrita and coming to the road where one turns left going up for about 60 metres. Then turn right up the road to Estaís and Jou. Follow this road all the way to Jou without going up the turning to Estaís.

1.45 Jou, 1306m. *There is water at Jou, either from the stream just before the village or from the spring at the trough, which is found by taking the first concrete ramp straight ahead as one arrives at the buildings. In springtime the Vallenda and Lledeto streams also should be flowing. Once almost derelict, Jou now is being restored, by new occupiers, to life again.* Follow the road through the bottom part of the village and take the signposted path down towards the Noguera Pallaresa valley on the right. Near the bottom, pass by a barn then through some inhabited buildings, taking the left branch of the road down into the village of...

2.20 La Guingueta d'Aneu, 945m. *Hotels with restaurant/bars, two camp sites one with shop for provisions. Some mountain equipment, including boots, can be obtained in Esterri d'Aneu, four kilometres to the N.* Take the sign-posted 'Dorbé' pista E, just to the left of the water point 'Font de Cyrille'. Turn right, S, on the other side of the Embalse de Torrassa. Very shortly take the obvious path ascending obliquely to the left with waymarks appearing a little later. Cross the fence and take the left branch, SE, following the waymarked track which makes a large zigzag to the west, some 15-20mins below the village. There is now no need to use the waymarked meadow on the final approach to the village as the track has been cleared of brambles. The first time in years! Overgrown again in 1999...

3.35 Dorbé, 1390m. *There is still one family living here and have been doing so at least twelve years, to my knowledge. In the square there is an important water point as no water will be found until well after the high pass.* Go between the buildings above the water point and turn right. Pass through the village and turn left N across two fields and then NW up a small rocky ridge. From here it is difficult to follow the waymarks as there are old ones and new ones all over the place and then none at all. The pass that we are aiming for is not the obvious one to the N but a small cleft that cannot be seen, exactly NE from Dorvé. High up NE there are two small clumps of birch which act as markers. Follow marks up the valley until large zigzags climb to the birch trees. These zigzags are not too clear as bikers have cut a more direct route. *Do spare some time to look back to see the view into the Noguera Pallaresa unfolding as height is gained.* Make your own way then to find the track way up above which gives easy access through the thickening undergrowth to the narrow pass of...

4.45 Collado de la Serra, 1740m. Turn right, E, and follow the delightfully clear path climbing easily through the wood on the north side of the ridge. *This is the northern spur of the west ridge from Calvo north.* About 30mins later, go SE up through some small meadows and then 10-15mins later, at an old water trough, climb E by zigzags then S to the crest of the ridge. Turn left, NE, to follow the ridge for a while before turning across the head of the valley on the right above Berrós Sobirà, seen way below, to leave the trees and reach...

6.05 Coll de Calvo, 2207m. *Splendid view into the National Park to the west. The path N goes to the obvious north summit of Calvo.* Go N for a few metres before turning down NE and then E. The route is quite easy to follow but it is important to locate waymarks after it becomes vague over grassy patches. Follow the marks down which turn S towards an old telegraph pole and just before reaching this, the trail goes SE to another tall pole with waymarks. A few minutes later turn E again at a small meadow to go down the ridge past a signpost, 'Dorbé'. A few more minutes later, well before the bottom of the ridge, look out for a path to the right going SSE which turns SW into a small valley turning SE after it crosses the stream. Follow the clear path SE then S to zigzag down the steep rocks to...

7.30 Estaon, 1240m. *Casa Pau, at the bottom of the rocks, no longer provides accommodation and meals. It may be possible to stay in a room of the old school just opposite but there are no other facilities. There are several water points, the lowest being perhaps the best quality. For camping it would be necessary to go down to the stream and a short way into next day's stage.*

Day 26: Estaon - Tavascan

Distance:	12.5 kilometres
Height gain:	630 metres
Height loss:	750 metres
Time:	4hrs 20mins

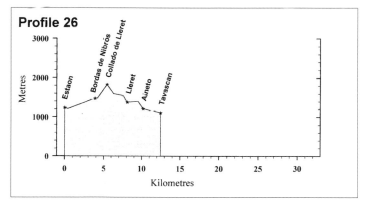

A much easier pastoral day past ancient remote farm buildings then steeply to the Coll de Lleret with the trail climbing to the top of the first crags beyond the village of Lleret. It follows an ancient track high above the valley of Noguera de Lladorre, sometimes crossing crags by dry stone engineering (care needed in places) before coming down to Aineto and Tavascan. There should be no problem with navigation but as this is a farming area, good water from Estaon should be carried.

Maps: *Editorial Alpina Pica d'Estats. IGN Carte de randonnées Couserans.*

Camping: *Wild camping after Estaon.*

0.00 Estaon, 1240m. From Casa Pau pass down the narrow passageway to the road below. Signpost to La Guingueta and Dorbé. Turn left, E, and follow the road down, turning NNE, to the Río d'Estahon. Cross the bridge and immediately climb up the earth bank to the left to reach a pista in a few metres. Turn left, N, and follow the pista along the left bank. 10-15mins later, at another bridge, the route goes straight on along an old path.

However, crossing the bridge and re-crossing the river again a little later the pista becomes a path across a field to join with the old route once more. The pista way is preferable in wet weather. Continue N along the path passing...

1.00 Bordas de Nibrós, 1480m. *There is one building that can be used for an overnight stop. Best place for a camp would be a little further on, keeping to the true left bank.* Continue N along the track but keep an eye out for the sharp turn back right, S, in about 3 minutes. Climb steeply up this path past a borda and then turn NE to reach another. Follow the marks around the left of this taking the left branch, E, of the path beyond. About 10 minutes later the path turns sharp left, N, for a while before turning SE to reach the pass...

2.00 Coll de Lleret, 1830m. Go a few metres NE, then a few more SSE and then, after a few more, turn down E to reach in 10mins a signpost 'Estaon-Tavascan'. The marks lead SSE to a rough pista and zigzag down, eventually turning N to reach more turns E to the NW edge of...

2.55 Lleret, 1381m. *Villagers helpful and camping possible.* Continue NNE to the stream, a short way from the village. Then turn left NNW up a path to cross the stream, continuing N on the other side to climb to the top of the first crags. Once located the trail more or less contours high up the side of the valley. Much later, just before Aineto, it drops down ENE very steeply and it is necessary to follow the waymarks closely to reach the pista going S then N at the entrance to the village of...

4.05 Aineto, 1220m. Go up the steep concrete road to the left, N, which turns E around the top of the village. Look out for the wide track cum pista to the left, N. Take this all the way to...

4.20 Tavascan, 1120m. *A small village with hotels, restaurants, bars, shop and telephone. Both food and small equipment shops will open upon request.*

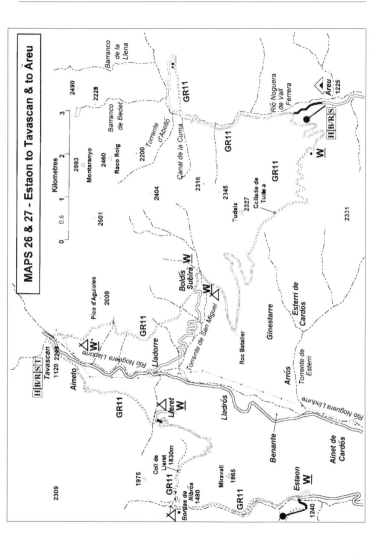

MAPS 26 & 27 - Estaon to Tavascan & to Àreu

Day 27: Tavascan - Àreu

Distance:	17.5 kilometres
Height gain:	1120 metres
Height loss:	1015 metres
Time:	6hrs 20mins

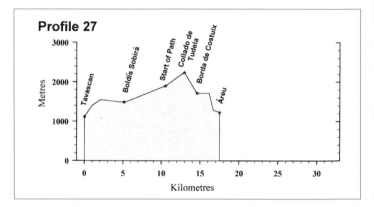

A steep haul through the woods above Tavascan leads to another high contouring path down the Noguera Lladorre valley. Then a long pista climb through more woods to gain access to the Esterri de Cardós valley with the pass at its head. Then steeply down to the pista above Àreu.

Maps: *Editorial Alpina Pica d'Estats. IGN Carte de randonnées Couserans.*

Camping: *Campsite at Àreu, open during the summer only. Possible at 'fuente' above Tavasacan and just beyond Boldís Sobirá.*

0.00 Tavascan, 1120m. Cross the bridge over the Río Noguera Lladorre turning left to find straightaway a waymarked track, on the right, climbing steeply up the line of a covered water channel. This crosses a pista and continues steeply to a small building to do with the water supply. Turn right, S, crossing the pista again and climb steeply through the birch wood. After some time the gradient eases and it comes to a small meadow which is passed on the left. This leads to another field which is also passed up on the left. The marks come to a fuente sign at a stone wall with a third grassy area above. *Possibility of a camp here.* Climb up through the trees on the left of this third meadow. Turn right, S, and follow this trail as it climbs to gain sufficient height to cross the side valley ahead above its steepest part. If the marks are lost, just keep climbing diagonally through the wood. Just before the gully take a right fork in the trail. Follow the clear path to the first fields above Boldís Sobirá where it becomes indistinct for a short distance. Here, go straight on, close to the stone wall on the left, and the way becomes clear again. Follow the path down to...

2.05 Boldís Subirà, 1480m. *Water point. 15 minutes into the next section, just after the pista on the left, which goes into the private property, look out for a water point on the right and place to camp.* From the northern part of the village take the pista E which crosses the Torrente de San Miguel and climbs SW through the trees towards the Roc de Bataller on the large W ridge of Tudela. Much later it turns back to the E and again turns SW. It turns to the E again and goes round another bend. Now, look out for the waymarked track off right, S, which climbs towards the S ridge of Tudela. The trail goes to the pass between two small hills, with small fenced enclosure, at the...

4.20 Coll de Tudela, 2243m. Go down SE into the wood where care should be taken to locate the waymarks as they zigzag down eastwards to reach the Bordas de Costuix, where the path passes between two buildings to become a pista, water point. Follow the pista down, SE then NE, through large bends to the road above Àreu. GR11 signpost Coll de Tudela-Tavascan. Turn right, S, following the road to...

6.20 Àreu, 1225m. *Hotel, restaurant, shop and campsite.*

Day 28: Àreu - Refugio de Baiau (J.M. Montfort)

Distance:	15.5 kilometres
Height gain:	1350 metres
Height loss:	60 metres
Time:	5hrs 30mins

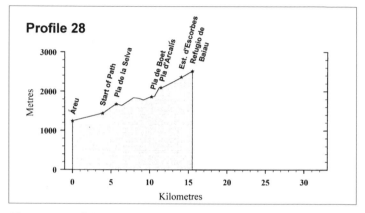

The crossing of the Port de Baiau tomorrow is a serious undertaking in bad weather or poor snow conditions early in the season. The danger is passing the two lakes on the Andorran side of the pass if the snow is deep and rotten. It can partly cover the lakes, masking the water's edge, and with the snow sloping steeply to the water, large blocks can break off into the lakes. Firm snow here is fine but in soft, rotten conditions it becomes both difficult and dangerous. There are two ways of overcoming this problem of rotten snow if it is essential to continue into Andorra. Either cross into Andorra by the HRP, which is lower than the GR11, via the pass to the north, Port de Boet, 2520 metres, with a brief passage down into France before ascending to cross the Port de Rat, 2542 metres, and into Andorra. Or, if the lake passage looks dicey, having crossed the Portella de Baiau, 2757 metres, it is possible to avoid it by climbing SE along the rocky ridge to the north, starting at a small pass ENE from the Portella, which reaches the summit of Pic Alt de Coma Pedrosa, 2942 metres. An easy ridge to those used to scrambling, continental route grade 1. From the summit go down the S ridge to where one can either come off right across easy snow well above the lower lake or take *the easy snow gully to the left and find the way down to the Coma Pedrosa. Normally the snow is good in the spring but poor conditions during May and early June of 1995 have prompted the above warning. For today there are no such worries, as the route passes through wooded valleys then climbs more steeply across open ground surrounded by high mountain wilderness. To the north lies the highest mountain in Cataluña, Pica d'Estats, 3143 metres, on a remote part of the border with France.*

Maps: *Editorial Alpina Pica d'Estats. IGN Carte de randonnées Haute-Ariège Andorre.*

Camping: *There are camping areas in the lower 'Plas' and opportunities to camp higher until the grass runs out. It is also possible to camp beyond the Refugio de Baiau, beside the lake, just before the climb to the pass.*

0.00 Àreu, 1225m. Leave the village by the road, N, which soon becomes a pista passing the left turn to the Coll de Tudela. In just under 3 kilometres turn right across the Rio Noguera de Vall Ferrera and continue N along the left bank for about 5 minutes before turning right, ENE, going up a path passing by stone walls and some bordas where the trail becomes grassy. It soon joins the main pista, which is crossed to take a steeply ascending track, which short cuts a large loop, to join the pista again just before...

1.40 Pla de la Selva, 1680m. *Camping no longer permitted.* Follow the left branch of the pista and some minutes later look out for a path right, E, going up into a pine plantation. Follow this and some time later it becomes a forest pista. 5-10 minutes later, take an undulating path, right, which goes down to join the main pista from Àreu again. Cross the pista to a path at a right hand bend, which allows a short cut, joining the pista above, or one can just follow the pista. As the pista turns SE towards the Pla de Boet there is a sign on the left and...

2.55 Path to Refugio de Vall Ferrera, 1840m. *The hut, guardian during the summer, lies 15-20mins to the north at 1940m. Take this path down to cross the stream for the Port de Boet route. Camping area in the Pla de Boet.* For the GR11, follow the pista SE above the Pla de Boet and in 10mins, where the pista turns sharp right, go straight on along a path SSE. The path climbs to another high

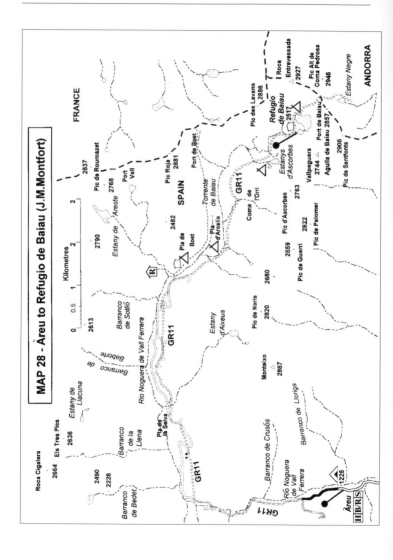

MAP 28 - Àreu to Refugio de Baiau (J.M.Montfort)

pasture, the Pla d'Arcalís, where it passes close to the stream, still on the left bank. It then climbs E, crossing a side stream, continues climbing ENE before turning SSE to reach...

4.55 Estany d'Ascorbes, 2360m. Pass the lakes on their E side passing through rocks and grass ESE then SSE, turning E to cross the stream coming from the Estany de Baiau and climb the steep rocky promontory to the hut...

5.30 Refugio de Baiau (J.M. Montfort), 2517m. *Metal hut perched on a promontory above the lake to the NW. In good condition, with kitchen area. Water from the lake.*

Day 29: Refugio de Baiau - Arans

Distance:	15.0 kilometres
Height gain:	750 metres
Height loss:	1905 metres
Time:	6hrs 10mins

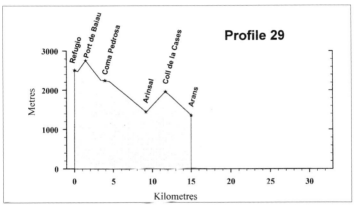

Today we pass into Andorra. The following information is provided to assist in your plans. The route from Arinsal to Encamp involves some very steep ups and downs. From Encamp to the east the gradients ease. Beyond Coma Pedrosa wild camping is difficult due to lack of water or sites. There is one campsite near Arans, at Ansalonga, complete with shop. There is a spot just south of and above La Cortinada where one could pitch a tent, if the above campsite is closed. The Tourist Office

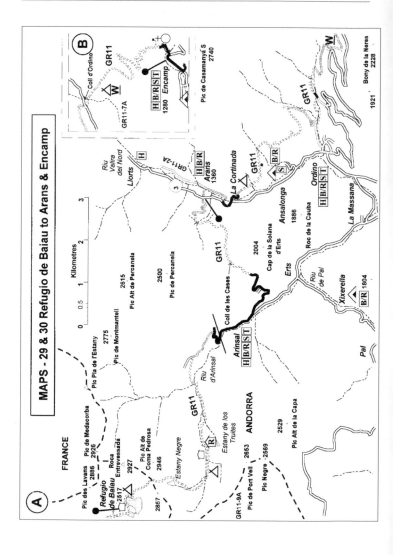

MAPS - 29 & 30 Refugio de Baiau to Arans & Encamp

advise using the excellent site at Xixerella (pronounced chi-cher-ray-ya). 3.5 kilometres from Arinsal by road, SE down to Erts then right, SSW, up to the campsite which is owned by a Cataluñan with British wife and staff. There is a bus service but it is probably quicker to walk. There is also a bus service from Arinsal to La Massana, Ordino, Arans, and down to Andorra la Viella. The route from La Cortinada to just above Ordino is pleasant enough but involves 400 metres of steep ascent and descent whereas the road route is much shorter and involves 60 metres down then up. There is a choice, then, of which way to go.

Maps: *Editorial Alpina Andorra. IGN Carte de randonnées Haute Ariège Andorre.*

Camping: *Ansalonga and Xixerella with bar and restaurant. See above.*

0.00 Refugio de Baiau, 2517m. From the hut go E down to the lake, continuing around the lake, cross a rock step and climb the first obvious grassy gully before turning SSE across the boulder field. Pick the best route to the steep loose section high above and

The GR11 on the Andorran side of the Port de Baiau (the lowest point, just left of centre). Dicey in these conditions

then ESE up the top very steep and loose scree section. Take care! I think that you will find that the most worn part is the easiest. This brings you to the high pass and border with Andorra at the...

1.10 Portella de Baiau, 2757m. *From here, one of Andorra's many GR routes follows the ridge to the right, the GR11-9A.* Go down easily SE then SSW to pass the upper lake, Estany Negre, on the left, E. Continue down, SSW, passing the lower lake on the left also. Cross the stream below, continuing down, S, to turn progressively E into the large hanging valley of Coma Pedrosa. The Refugio of the same name can be seen above the trail to the right beside Estany de los Truites. Go down E to the mouth of the valley passing a cabin over on the left suitable for an overnight stop. *From the mouth of the valley the Refugio de Coma Pedrosa, 2260m, lies above to the south.* Go down E into a small, delightful hollow to cross to the right of the stream coming from the Estany de los Truites. Follow the right of the stream down steeply into the wood. Much later the path turns N and comes to a junction of streams called the Aigües Juntes. These are crossed by two small footbridges. Follow the path on the other side generally E to reach a pista above, which is followed to the road. *There is a huge avalanche protection wall ahead, right across the valley.* Turn right following the road steeply down, turning SE to pass through the wall by a road and foot tunnel into...

4.00 Arinsal, 1466m. *Hotels, restaurants, and shop on the left just before the road to the left 'Carretera Mas Ribafreta'. This is the wide road that forks left towards the bottom of the town.* Turn left up this road, SE, and follow the road as it turns left, passing some flats and turns back SE again. A short time later take the path left, sign-posted 'Cami de Coll de les Cases', and, if it is overgrown, continue up the pista for 80 metres as it turns left to join with the path. Clear marks lead the way steeply up through the wood by zigzags, generally in a NNE direction, turning NE to the grassy pass of...

5.15 Coll de les Cases, 1965m. Go down NNE over grass to locate waymarks on trees that lead down a wooded gully ENE then ESE. After about 15-20mins, leave the gully, E then N, and a few minutes later it turns NW. Five minutes later leave a grassy track to the right but go down left to cross a stream going up NE on

Camping in the Como Pedrosa

the other side to cross another stream. A few more minutes later, take a right turn, E, which leads to a pista going NNE. Follow this as it turns back S to join a road which winds its way down into...

6.10 Arans, 1360m. *Small hamlet with hotel, bar/restaurants, but no shop.*

Day 30: Arans - Encamp

Distance:	14.5 kilometres
Height gain:	1010 metres
Height loss:	1090 metres
Time:	4hrs 45mins
Start:	See map

The route follows the left of the Valira del Nord river down to the next village before climbing along the lower SW flank of Casamanya to overlook Ordino before descending to within a short distance from it. See introduction to yesterday's stage. Then by a complex mix of pistas and paths, well marked and not difficult to follow, it climbs to the Coll

143

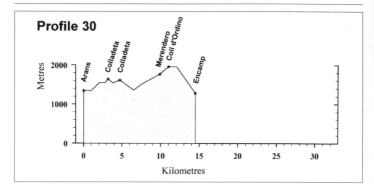

d'Ordino. *Across grass and through woods to the very steep descent past terraces to the town of Encamp, seen and heard below.*

Maps: *Editorial Alpina Andorra. IGN Carte de randonnées Haute-Ariège Andorre.*

Camping: *Campsite at Encamp. Possibility of camping just below the Coll d'Ordino in the early part of the season when water is present.*

0.00 Arans, 1360m. Cross the road, E, and go down beside the restaurant La Font d'Arans, to cross the river Valira del Nord. The GR11-2A joins from the left. Turn right, S, and go along the pista. About 10mins later, cross the bridge on the right to join the road, turning left down to...

0.15 La Cortinada, 1340m. *Hotel, bar/restaurant and shop.* Go E across another bridge to the old part of the village and follow narrow streets, SE, SW, SE and finally NE, to find a pista (probably a road now) going up SE to some houses. Go past the buildings, cross a chain and the pista becomes a path. About 3mins later there is a small meadow above on the left suitable for a tent with a stream 100m further on. Cross the stream taking the left, S, fork which zigzags steeply up through the trees, later to contour past a farm on the right to another stream. From the second stream, about 40mins from La Cortinada, go up again steeply by zigzags, SE then SSE. About 30mins from the second stream, the trail turns sharp left, E, on the final climb. *Viewpoint overlooking Ordino.* In 15mins or so the trail arrives at a pista. Turn

Leaving the Estós hut (Day 20)

Estany Gargulles in the Circ de Colomers just west of the large
Obago lake (Day 23)

Estany del Port de Ratera (Day 24)
The GR 11 trail beside the Estany Long (Day 24)

right and go steeply down, S then SW, turning sharply E and at the bottom, it turns to the W...

2.05 Junction to Ordino, 1360m. *The pista continues down to Ordino in about 10mins where there are all the usual services, including a shop for provisions upon entering the town.* Now for the climb to the Coll d'Ordino. Take the ascending waymarked path E, ignoring a path climbing to the right, and in about 7mins it turns left across a stream, climbing NW to the top of the bank, then turns right, NE. Ten minutes later cross the stream to the right, turning left, E, up to a pista. Turn left, NE, along the pista, crossing the stream again, with the waymarks leading off the pista to a trail to the left, more or less parallel to it. The waymarked route crosses this pista to follow a path soon to cross a stream by a wooden bridge on the right, E, then turning left, N, for a few metres before turning back S and then E to climb beside another stream. Five minutes later it climbs to the terminus of a pista. Turn right, SW, and in a few minutes take the obvious steeply climbing pista to the left, SW turning E. *This climbs to a picnic area beside the road in about 30mins.* Shortly before the picnic area, take a left branch which climbs even steeper with the gradient assuaged by a path which, within a few metres, turns off left, E, then turns back across the steep pista and then up E to...

3.10 Merendero, 1780m. *Water available but with limited flow, 1999.* Go up S by the path to the left of the wire fenced compound to join an old pista climbing E. This pista, with a final bend to the SW, arrives at the road a few metres below...

3.35 Coll d'Ordino, 1970m. Cross the road and go up over grass to the high point and orientation table. *Signpost 'Les Bons 1hr 30mins'. The GR11-7A crosses here, climbing over the Pic de Casamanyá to gain the enticing ridges to the north. Another day perhaps!* Go down SE, just left of an obvious level path, to find a grassy pista which is followed SE. It becomes indistinct as it crosses a boggy area (in springtime) where it is possible to camp if water is still flowing in the small stream. A clear path is followed as it enters the wood, SE. This turns SW before turning slightly left to descend very steeply past terraced fields, generally SE. The route is well marked, leading ENE to a stream at one point and about 15mins later, as the path turns E again just before a building, look out for a turn right, S. Follow the path down to the small Ermita de Sant Roma, over the rocky path down to the road Carrer de Sant Roma, over the bridge Pont de les Bons, turning right down the Avenida de Rouillac to...

4.45 Encamp, 1280m. *Fairly large town with all services and campsite. Continue down the main road SW about 600m, then turn right to the Town Park, which once was 'Camping Meritxell'. Turn left and about 150m from the park, turn left into 'Camping International'.*

Day 31: Encamp - Cabana dels Esparvers

Distance:	20.5 kilometres
Height gain:	1350 metres
Height loss:	560 metres
Time:	6hrs

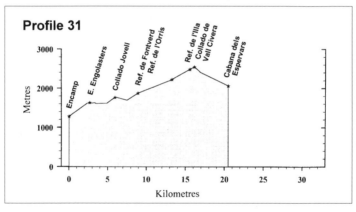

The Riu Madriu valley remains, for the present, the only main valley in Andorra not containing a road or pista. There are plans to change this state of affairs but there is also a strong anti-road lobby from within Andorra. The road that has been laid from Les Escaldes to Estany d'Engolasters just passes the entrance and only a few hundred metres are used by the GR11. The Madriu, though surrounded by high mountains, has a gentle ambience. Running water and many camping spots no doubt help. This really is a pleasant and civilised walk into walkers-only territory with morning coffee at Estany d'Engolasters

before the gentle walk over the small pass into the long, easy Madriu valley. Soon all the bustle of town and road is forgotten in this idyllic haven of peace and tranquillity. Popular for walkers and fly fishermen.

Maps: *Editorial Alpina Andorra. IGN Carte de randonnées Haute-Ariège Andorre.*

Camping: *There are many places to camp in the Riu Madriu valley when the trail passes near to the river. On the other side of the pass one can camp below the first part of the descent and beyond the stone huts of Esparvers down by the stream.*

0.00 Encamp, 1280m. From 'Camping International', turn right and right again, passing the park, to the main road. Turn left and in about 150m, cross the main road and take the road that turns left round the building with an outside spiral concrete pedestrian way on its left. Follow it around to the left of the building to find a pista behind. Turn right, WSW, along the pista, ignore a grassy track left but take an ascending pista to the left, S, by a telephone

Mid-June in Andorra! On the approach to the GR11 at Encamp from France, through the Vall d'Incles

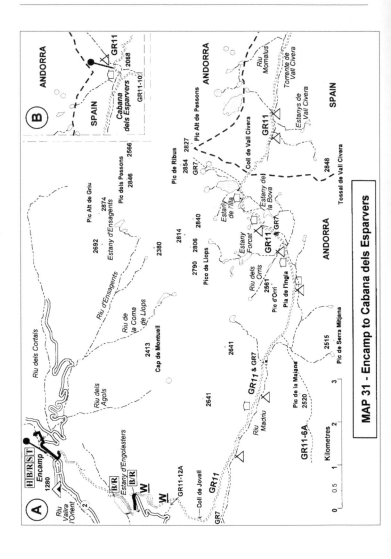

MAP 31 - Encamp to Cabana dels Esparvers

line, about 4 minutes from the road. 3 minutes later it becomes a path, W then SW. Some minutes later ignore a path to the left but carry straight on W with a short turn to the left, SE, before continuing, generally SSW to the northern end of...

1.05 Estany d'Engolasters, 1616m. Cross the chain to new bar/restaurant above to the left. Take the pista around the SE side of the lake to the dam at the other end. Just after the dam, take a path E and in a few minutes it arrives at a car parking area and bar/restaurant at the end of the road which comes up from Les Escaldes. Go down the road, ENE, to the first sharp bend to the right. Ignore signs of a track to the left, NNE, but take the pista further round the bend, which leaves to the left, SE. Very soon this passes a pista to the right, then a water point. A few minutes later the pista divides. One way goes up left, over the small ridge ahead. Take the one going straight on through a small tunnel. Another water point is reached shortly and soon after, the pista becomes a path going SSE, soon to reach a picnic area and further water point. The trail is soon joined from the right by the GR11-12A and climbs the short distance to...

1.40 Coll de Jovell, 1780m. Cross the pass, SW, to pick up the path steeply descending to the ESE which is joined at the bottom by the GR7 coming from the right, before climbing along the right of the Riu Madriu. Some time later take the left branch of the path SE. Still climbing, the trail passes through a gate and shortly arrives at...

2.30 Refugio de Fontverd, 1880m. *Good hut suitable for overnight stop, 6 places. Beware of especially aggressive mosquitoes at some of the obvious picnic spots by the river.* The track climbs clearly along the north side of the river, ESE, leaving it for a short while, SE, as the river makes a bend to the south. It joins the river again upon entering the high pasture, Pla de l'Ingla, with a small cabin to the right over a log bridge. Continue across the meadow climbing ENE and in a few minutes arrive at the...

3.45 Refugio del Riu dels Orris, 2230m. *Good hut with 6 places and spring a few metres away to the NW. Camping close by.* Follow the marks as they turn towards the NE passing small lakes and more camping places and a hut after about 35mins. Ten minutes later cross a log bridge turning SE then NE again to reach...

4.40 Refugio de l'Illa, 2485m. *Large and now extended unmanned hut.* From the east of the hut take the ascending path to the large lake above. Take the right fork, E, to easily reach the...

4.55 Coll de Vall Civera, 2550m. Go SE down to the left bank of a stream. A little later the path crosses the stream and returns to the left bank shortly turning E then SE towards the bottom of the valley. *The mountain ridge ahead is that enclosing the south side of Vall Civera but as the trail turns to the E, tomorrow's route is seen ahead. It would be a good idea to make a mental note of its geography to aid navigation. The route will climb into the hanging valley seen above the tree line, ESE, with the pass, just beyond the head of this valley, to the left.* Keep to the right of a grassy ridge to pick up the trail a little lower. Follow this down to cross to the right bank some time later. Take care now to keep an eye out for the point where the GR11 turns down left from the GR11-10. Waymarks and sign on the right. Cross the stream where possible (the footbridge has collapsed) and go up NNE to locate the small stone built cabin...

6.00 Cabana dels Esparvers, 2068m. *Small stone cabin with very narrow entrance, 2 or 3 places.* Take the ascending path E to find the descent to the river, reached in a few minutes, where one can camp.

Day 32: C. dels Esparvers - Refugio de Malniu

Distance:	10.3 kilometres
Height gain:	810 metres
Height loss:	740 metres
Time:	4hrs

A steep climb before the gradient eases to the Portella. Very steep descent, then by lakes and through boulders and meadows, with some care needed to locate the Refugio Engorgs.

Maps: *Editorial Alpina Cerdanya.*

Camping: *Places can be found by the lakes below the pass and before the Refugio Engorgs in the small valley above. No camping is allowed at the Refugio de Malniu because of the proximity of the pista, so a spot needs to be found well before the hut.*

0.00 Cabana dels Esparvers, 2068m. *An old route used to go north from here before climbing back southwards to gain the hanging valley*

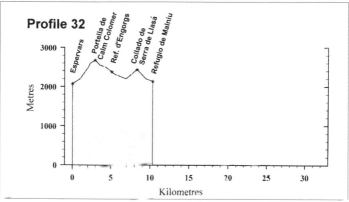

Profile 32

before the pass. Other waymarks can be found in the wood to the east. The better part of an afternoon was spent investigating the lower part of the ascent without being absolutely certain of the current way. From the bothy, go up the grassy rise to the east to locate the path with clear marks going down to and crossing the stream. Height has to be gained in the wood ahead. Marks leading farther north might lead back into this wood. However, go a few metres S by the left bank of the stream, turning SE to climb to a large grassy area. The clear path vanishes but carry straight on SE across the grass, with the trees on the left, towards the trees on the other side. A SE course should locate an isolated boulder with a waymark, but not located in 1999. Keep a look out for a grassy ramp that climbs back, NNW, into the wood. Follow this until the gradient eases and further height can be gained by climbing tracks through the undergrowth. It winds its way upward in an easterly direction to a clear waymarked path above. The path goes SE and in a few minutes turns N to grass and then E to a cairned boulder. A few minutes later it climbs SE again turning E into the hanging valley. The path crosses to the other side of the valley climbing its left side, ENE. 5 minutes later the route turns sharply right, S, to reach the top of the valley side. Ignore a waymark on a large rock on the right but turn gradually left, ENE, to reach the obvious low saddle ahead...

1.30 Portella de Calm Colomer, 2680m. *Fine views. The other side*

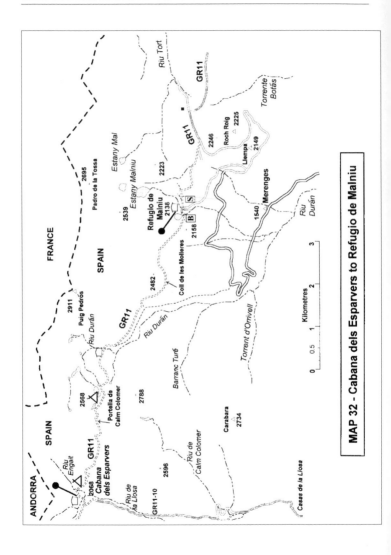

MAP 32 - Cabana dels Esparvers to Refugio de Malniu

is extremely steep. Remaining snow is also steep and although fairly easy to climb in good condition it can be rather daunting to descend. It can be avoided by using rocks on the left. It is essential not to descend further from below these rocks, as the ground below is treacherous. Cross the slope beneath the snow to continue the descent over scree to the south and to where waymarks appear again. Without the hazard of snow, follow waymarks to the right, SE, which lead diagonally across the slope, passing over a small rocky ridge, before reaching easier ground. Continue SE until the route turns NE for a while, becoming unclear. Do not go straight on over the low ridge ahead but turn SSE around it; follow a faint path turning NE to arrive at the head of a small valley. Follow the valley down, E, to...

2.15 Refugio Engorgs, 2375m. *Hut in very good condition with table, fireplace and first aid kit Room for 12-18 people. Water from the stream.* Go down SE to cross the Riu Duran, going S then SE, around the grassy area on the other side. Keep to the right and do not climb the steep edge but locate the steeply descending path. Shortly, take the left branch, SE. The one on the right goes down to Meranges. Ascend a little, to pass the lower slopes of the SW ridge of Puig Pedros, before continuing the descent SE. Cross various streams, at one boggy place by fallen tree, climb to the left to find the trail, which climbs S then E to a Collado on the ridge called Serra de Llasa. Go down, NE then E, leaving the trees behind with the picnic area below in view. Go down the fields to a wooden bridge crossing the stream coming from the Estany Sec, which leads to the car parking area and...

4.00 Refugio de Malniu, 2138m. *Large hut with guardian during the summer, accommodating 40, bar and small shop available at this time for expensive refreshments and provisions. Due to access by pista, this is very busy during the holiday period with such delightful scenery to the north.*

Day 33: Refugio de Malniu - Puigcerdà

Distance:	15 kilometres
Height gain:	95 metres
Height loss:	1030 metres
Time:	3hrs 20mins

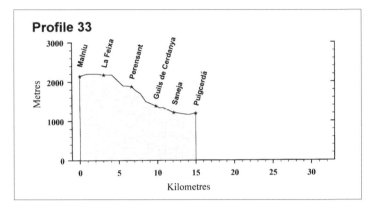

The GR11 makes its way down from the mountains to the high plateau area around Puigcerdà. The route is fairly well marked though some care is needed in the grassy places and at the start. An easy day swinging down paths and pistas.

Maps: *Editorial Alpina Cerdanya.*

Camping: *Camping Pirineus, just beyond Seneja, does not open until the end of June, unfortunately. The campsite beyond Puigcerdà should be open all year. It would be possible to camp near the water canal just before point 1750. Puigcerdà provides the only other accommodation.*

0.00 Refugio de Malniu, 2138m. Go down across the pista bridge turning left, E, along an old trail which climbs through the wood towards the Estany Malniu. Seven minutes later take the right branch, E, and then in a couple of minutes ignore the waymarks, continuing straight on to the lake, but look out for a turning to the right climbing S, also through the trees, not so clearly marked. The trail turns to the E losing a little height. It goes across a stream and passes a pond to the left. When a rough pista comes

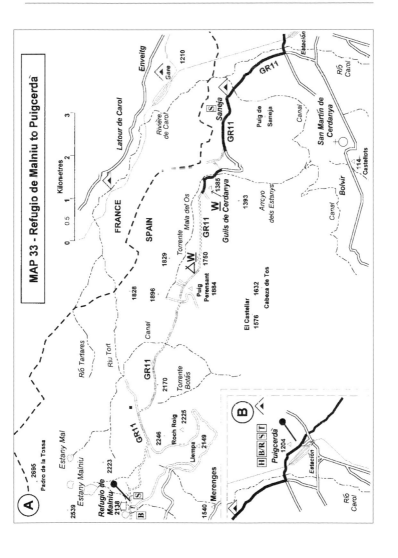

MAP 33 - Refugio de Malniu to Puigcerdà

from the right, keep on SE a few metres to another pista, then E across an open grassy area with the line of a large pista seen to the right. Continue E to join the main pista and follow it NE to within sight of the Refugio de Feixa over on the left. Before reaching the Refugio, keep a look out for marks indicating the place to turn right across grass to soon pick up a grassy pista going SE. Continue along this pista which turns E, ignoring a branch to the left. Four minutes later it becomes indistinct across grass, but continue SE and in 5mins the pista is clear again going ESE soon turning E. It becomes unclear again at another grassy place where, ignoring a waymark on the right, follow vehicle tracks to the left which turn SE. Go across the main pista ahead. *This is the one that comes from Malniu past the Refugio de Feixa.* Go across grass, ESE, to find the pista going down into the wood. Pass two pistas to the left a few minutes later and in a few more minutes pass through a fence and on down to an open grassy area. Cross a small stream issuing from the small canal on the left and go up the ridge E, passing a rocky outcrop on the left, though either side will do. Continue steeply down the ridge, E, by a stony gully. Much later, as the path becomes indistinct over grass, ignore a farm pista slightly below to the right, but continue straight on, slightly north of east, to cross a stream. Continue E and down to the pista on the left below. This becomes a road and soon take the left fork which turns to the right and a little later turn left to the main square of...

2.05 Guils de Cerdanya, 1385m. *Water point in Main Square, no other amenities.* Take the SE exit from the square down to the main road. Go along the road about 300m and where it bends to the right carry straight on along a pista, SE. At the junction ahead turn right, SSE, down to the road again. Turn left, E, and follow all the way to...

2.35 Seneja, 1220m. *Small shop behind the church.* Pass through the village on to the main road again, passing Camping Pirineus over on the left. *When open, this site has a bar/restaurant and shop.* Follow the main road SE to cross, E, the large bridge over the Río Carol. The road winds its way to the SE again. *Bar/restaurant here.* Continue along the road SE to the railway station square where steps to the left, NE, climb to...

3.20 Puigcerdà, 1204m. *All services are to be found here.* If the town is not required, continue SE from the station to the main road and the turning to Age.

Day 34: Puigcerdà - Planoles

Distance:	26.5 kilometres
Height gain:	1020 metres
Height loss:	1085 metres
Time:	7hrs

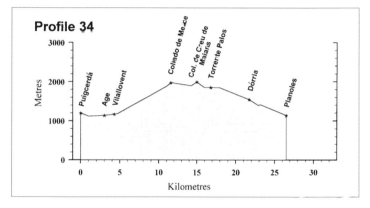

A long day. The only real possibility of making it shorter is to camp in a meadow just before the Torrente de Punt Turo above Dórria. The route uses the road to just beyond Vilallovent and then climbs to a little pass to gain entry to a narrow valley which is ascended along its right bank, eventually reaching the floor of the valley. A pista is then followed for a while before turning to climb to the border and then the long descent by pista to Dórria and old trail to Planoles. Waymarking is not all that it should be and it can be confusing on the border ridge in cloud. It is hoped, therefore, that users of this guide will find much time saved. In order to avoid drinking from woodland streams, water will have to be carried.

Maps: *Editorial Alpina Cerdanya.*

Camping: *There are no campsites but a good place can be found in the*

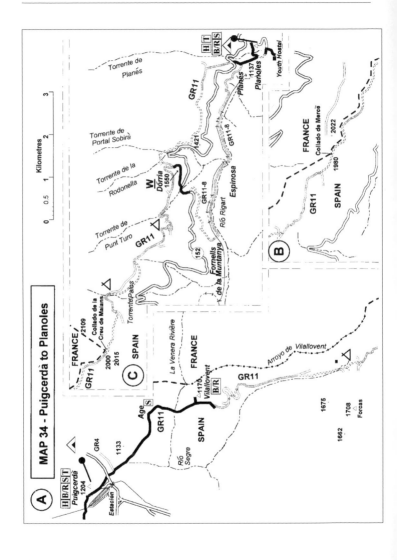

MAP 34 - Puigcerdà to Planoles

meadow just beside the Torrente de Punt Turo. It might also be possible to find a spot in the wood where the trail crosses the small stream below the house marked on the sketch map. It might also be possible where the pista crosses the Torrente Palos. There is a campsite above Planoles.

0.00 Puigcerdà, 1204m. Go down through the town, SE, to find steps and roads which lead to the main road below. Then locate the small road opposite, about 200m E of the railway bridge, signposted to Age and going SE. Soon avoid a waymarked pista on the left, the GR4, but continue along the road SE. Climb steeply through Age where there is a shop. Pass by the turning left to...

0.45 Vilallovent, 1170m. *There is a bar/restaurant here.* A few minutes S along a cement road, take the unlikely very steep earth pista (very muddy when wet) that climbs SW turning S then E. A few minutes after it has turned E, keep a look out for a path to the right. Take the path ESE which turns S to soon arrive at the pista again. Turn right and soon left onto a path that arrives at a small pass and pista. Turn left, E, and follow the pista as it turns S climbing the right of the tree filled valley. The pista has been extended, so after about 20 mins look out for a track going straight on, as the pista turns to the left. Follow the path S, avoiding a grassy pista to the right. A few minutes later avoid a path to the right but go on S turning SE then S again soon to reach a large pista. Cross the pista to pick up one beyond travelling SE. Follow this for about 2 kilometres before, at a right bend, go up steeply left, SE. Bear left slightly towards the top to reach the border with France and border stone (BS) No. 500 at...

3.00 Collado de Mercè, 1980m. *In fact the border fence and ditch do not follow the line of the border stones here. So, in cloud, if the way is not known, and not grasped from the maps, there can be considerable confusion, especially after BS 501-II.* In misty conditions, from BS 500 go ESE across grass just below the high ground with BS 501-I below to the right. This bearing should bring you to the fence, ditch and cattle grid gate in the fence by BS 501-II in less than 10 minutes. *On a clear day follow the path SE from BS 500, then NE to the same point.* Do not follow the obvious path SE into the trees below the fence but go across the grass SE below the trees to locate a waymark on a boulder only seen when standing to the south side of the BS 501-II, as the rock is mostly hidden by a bush. A waymarked pista soon appears which is followed down SE into the trees past BS 501-III. The pista soon becomes a path passing BS501-IV, 501-V and at 501-VI a new pista, which has mostly obliterated the old path, is climbed steeply S to reach BS 502. Cross the fence line ahead, memorial cross on the right...

3.50 Collado de la Creu de Maians, 2000m. *There is no longer a clear way down from here and all guides are vague. It is necessary to descend slightly south of east to cut a pista about 100m below and about 700m distant.* Go down E across grass to the obvious hollow which becomes a narrow grassy gully where a waymark can be located. From this mark either take the track going into the wood E and find easy ways down through the trees, without difficulties, always on an E bearing, until the pista is reached, or try following the gully. Turn left, NE, following the pista to cross the Torrente de Palos, turning then SE. A waymarked path is followed now, below and instead of the pista and about 50mins later the Torrente de Punt Turo is reached. *Camping spot just above the pista to the left, before the stream.* Continue along the pista SE which turns to the N then S before coming to the road below...

5.35 Dórria, 1550m. *The GR11-8 continues straight on down the road and might be considered as an alternative if this already long day is being split. The next section of the GR11 is overgrown with occasional thorns and brambles and needs clearing. It is quite manageable in dry conditions but in the wet it is very unpleasant and either the GR11-8 or the main road would be a good choice, though both of these add over 2kms.* The GR11 turns sharp left, N, from the green rubbish container, down a pista to the stream below. Cross the stream and on to another, the Torrente de Portal Sobira, which is very slippery. **TAKE CARE!** Follow the old trail first SSE then turning E to cross a small pass before continuing down SE then E. With joy, it becomes a pista and in a few minutes turn right steeply down S, with the pista becoming a cement road joining the main road. Cross the road beside the Hostal de la Carretera and go down S though Planes. If going directly to the Youth Hostel, take the path and steps on the right as the road turns to go down N. Otherwise, follow the road down to the river then E across the bridge and up steeply, ENE, into...

7.00 Planoles, 1137m. *There is a small hotel (fonda), Youth Hostel near the railway station below the town. Bar/Restaurant and shops for provisions. The campsite 'Can Fosset' is above the town beside tomorrow's route.*

Day 35: Planoles - Núria

Distance:	21 kilometres
Height gain:	1600 metres
Height loss:	770 metres
Time:	6hrs 30mins

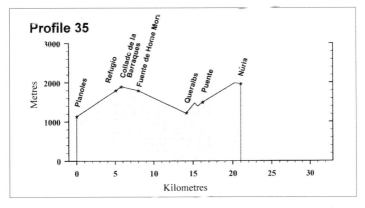

This day involves quite a bit of ascent. However, it could be split by staying at Queralbs or by camping above Dórria during the previous day and the camping spot during this day. The climb from Planoles is pleasant enough, though hard when off-road. All in all a varied and pleasing walk culminating in the climb along the Río Núria gorge.

Maps: *Editorial Alpina Cerdanya, and Puigmal.*

Camping: *It is possible to camp near the Fuente del Home Mort and there is a terraced camping area behind the Núria complex to the NNW with toilets and showers on the west side of the bar below. The camping ground has been prepared with fine gravel and takes pegs with difficulty, so some protection for groundsheets is required and rocks help with pitching. There is plenty of grass about but for decoration only.*

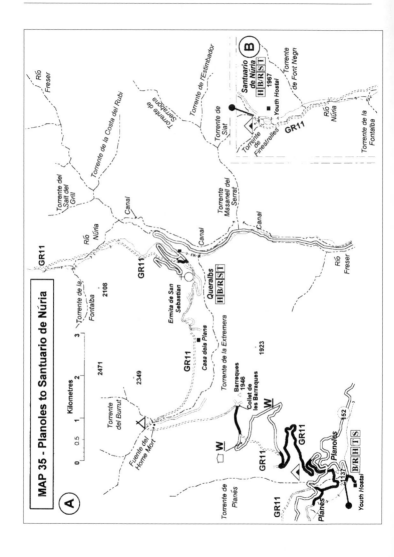

MAP 35 - Planoles to Santuario de Núria

The rack and pinion railway from Queralbs to Núria

0.00 Planoles, 1137m. *There are two cement roads going north from the main road above the town. The GR11 takes the westerly one. The tarmac road curving up to the main road reaches the east one, with the GR11 route just out of sight to the left.* From the bar/restaurant follow the tarmac road up to the main road. Ignore the concrete road ahead. Turn left and in a few metres turn right, N, up the cement road. Or, from the main square take one of the streets left, N, to locate the GR. A few minutes along the cement road take the right branch, NE, and in a few more minutes it climbs steeply to join a tarmac road above. *This comes from the other cement road via a long detour.* Turn left, NW, and follow this narrow road as it serpentines upward, passing Camping Can Fosset. About 3km later, while travelling NW, it makes a hairpin turn back SE, with a pista leaving to the N. *The small short cut across this bend is no longer in use.* Follow the bend around and in a few minutes take the waymarked route off to the left, NNE, which climbs steeply up through the forest. *The road continues to the same spot above but is very much longer though much easier.* The trail arrives at the road, crosses it and continues to climb NNE soon reaching a water point and picnic area with hut to the left.

1.45 Refugio, 1810m. *The Refugio has become dirty again as the doors have been left open and livestock have entered. From above the hut the GR11, for some unaccountable reason, used to climb NE to a ridge and come down to the collado but now no longer does so.* From the hut go up to the road and follow it E to...

2.00 Collet de les Barraques, 1890m. End of road and junction of pistas. Go down the one to the NW which turns to the N and in 10 minutes comes to a grassy place. The trail has now been clearly marked, going straight on, slightly W of N. It passes through trees to easily descend to the...

2.40 Crossing of the Torrente de la Extremera, 1800m. *Camping possible here.* Cross the river, go along a trail SSE to the pista, in about 6mins and almost immediately take the waymarked path going down to the right, SSE. At various junctions the route usually goes right. 20 minutes later, after a stream, at a grassy place, go SE to pick up the path again passing a small hut over on the left. In another 20 minutes a farm on the right is passed. Go down E, with the farm pista to the right, to join it and pass around a bend to take a short-cut off left, NNE. This joins with the pista again shortly, crosses a bridge over the stream and continues SE then E for about a kilometre. Then keep an eye out for a new route, a waymarked path that leads to...

4.00 Queralbs, 1220m. *Hotels, bars, restaurants, telephone and shops for provisions. NB. The shop tends to close, for the afternoon, well before 2pm. These services are found in the lower part of town to the south, below which lies the station of the rack railway to Núria or down to Ribes de Freser and the main line.* Return to the upper road by cobbled streets and turn right for a short way before taking the pista N, signposted Cami de Núria. Shortly, at a branch, take the pista ascending left, NNE, which looks as though it is only the access to the house seen above. Leave the house to the right and the pista becomes stony then later turns into a path which reaches a road. Turn right for a few metres before turning off left, continuing the climb up the path, N. The railway comes into view below on the right and the trail continues beside it for a while before crossing to the other side as the track passes into a tunnel.

Núria, once a monastery, now a luxury holiday complex

The path then goes down to the Río Núria to cross it by the Pont del Cremat to continue the ascent of the left side of the valley gaining height by zigzags in the gorge. After the gradient has eased the trail passes beneath the track by a small tunnel to continue climbing along the right side. Much later the path leads to the top of the last hill called Creu d'en Riba. *Somehow the railway track has managed to avoid climbing this last obstacle. I expect that you also will be stunned at what you see. A huge manmade ski and holiday complex, surrounded by such striking beauty, in the middle of nowhere.* Go down to cross the Torrente de Finestrelles to arrive at...

6.30 Santuario de Núria, 1967m. *Hotel with restaurant, two bars, shop and rack railway station adjacent. Camping area to NW with nearby cafe, toilets and showers. Youth Hostel above by cable car. Cheap meals can be had in the main bar.*

Day 36: Núria - Setcases

Distance:	21 kilometres
Height gain:	1080 metres
Height loss:	1770 metres
Time:	6hrs 20mins

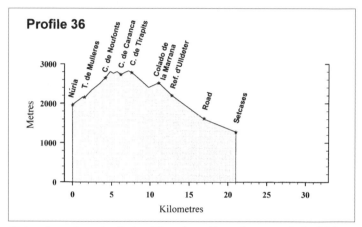

Today is unique in that, although well to the east of the highest mountains, the GR11 attains its greatest height as it passes along the border ridge for over 3km with extensive views in clear weather. This ridge could be difficult to navigate in cloud and even more so in cloud with snow covering. No such problems in good weather.

Maps: *Editorial Alpina Puigmal.*

Camping: *No official camping areas after Núria though places can be found up to 2400m.*

0.00 Santuario de Núria, 1967m. From behind the complex go NE to cross a small stone bridge and then follow the marks across grass and up a steep bank to join the ascending pista which is followed NE. *The valley to the north goes to the Collado d'Eina.* The pista becomes a path which leads into the Torrente de las Mulleres de Noucreus valley. At the entrance, a little below to the left, is a wooden bridge. *This was broken but usable during my visits.* Cross the bridge and go a few metres up NW to locate the

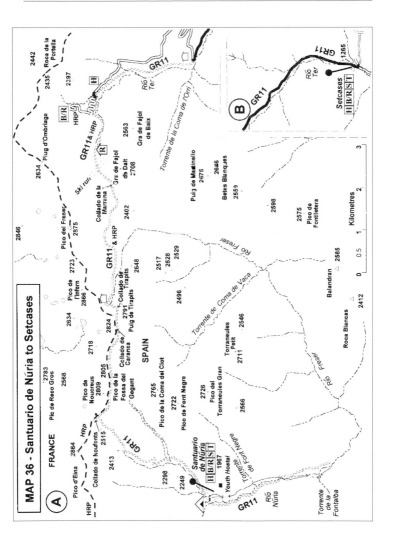

MAP 36 - Santuario de Núria to Setcases

trail climbing to the right by a series of large zigzags. The route is clearly marked as it climbs to the left side of the Torrente de Noufonts valley, at first in a northerly direction and then NE. A clear path climbs the final scree slope to…

1.45 Collado de Noufonts, 2645m. *Joined by the HRP from the left.* Turn right and climb the ridge SE passing a small stone shelter seen to the left. *Igloo type, useful as shelter in bad weather.* Over the summit ridge of Pico de Noucreus, 2809m, the route turns to the E down to the Collado de Noucreus. Then turning ESE and then NE to gain Pico de la Fossa del Gegant, 2805m. Down ESE to the Collado de Carenca, 2730m. Up again ESE to the west part of the next high section, the Pic Superior de la Vaca, 2824m, though it can be avoided to the right before reaching the summit. *(This summit is the highest point on the GR11.)* From here leave the ridge turning to the right, E, and with little descent reach…

3.00 Collado de Tirapits, 2791m. *If the descent looks too intimidating in snow, an easy descent over grass can be found to the north, NNE from Pic Superior de la Vaca.* Go down steeply N and then continue E across the hanging valley, passing a small stream at about 2400m, before climbing the pass to the E, between Puig de Bastiments to the NW and Pic Gra de Fajol to the SE, called…

3.55 Collado de la Marrana, 2520m. *Care is needed, early in the season.* **Beware of cornices!** *In snow, the trail contours from the right of the pass to descend the right side of the valley below. Once in the valley, the route goes down easily and across a wide ski piste to…*

4.25 Refugio de Ull de Ter, 2200m. *Guardian during the summer with bar and meals. Bothy for 10 open all year.* **(Cabin locked in the Spring of 1997.)** Continue E from the hut crossing the stream below by a small plank bridge. The path arrives at the road and, avoiding a steep gully on the right, go down easily, with the road zigzags on the left. At the last bend of the road, above a large parking area, follow the road down to cross the river and immediately take the trail on the right (waymarks eventually appear). If using the bar/restaurant seen below the bridge, there is a track beside the power pylon that goes down to the GR11. Follow the track down the left side of the river for about 3 kilometres where it passes a hut over on the left, in good condition, before the now wide track meets the road again at a hairpin bend. Follow the road, ESE at first, which follows the river Ter, crossing to the right side just before arriving at...

6.20 Setcases, 1265m. *Hotels, bar/restaurants, shop and telephone.*

Day 37: Setcases - Beget

Distance:	22 kilometres
Height gain:	820 metres
Height loss:	1575 metres
Time:	6hrs 30mins

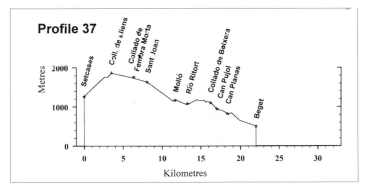

The higher mountains behind, we enter a more verdant region today and the highlight must be the long descent from the Collado de Lliens across grassy ridges down to Molló. Unless one has excellent navigation skills it would be well not to cross the ridges in mist or cloud. Water needs to be carried for the high section until supplies can be replenished at Molló.

Maps: *Editorial Alpina Costabona.*

Camping: *In the meadows below Beget.*

0.00 Setcases, 1265m. From the E of town cross the bridge over the river Ter taking the concrete road to a steep, rough pista on the right, climbing E. Slightly to the right, at a junction, continue up the remaining original path. Keep an eye out for the marks when it comes to grassy places and beware of biting flies. The following gives a quick reference to the direction in which to

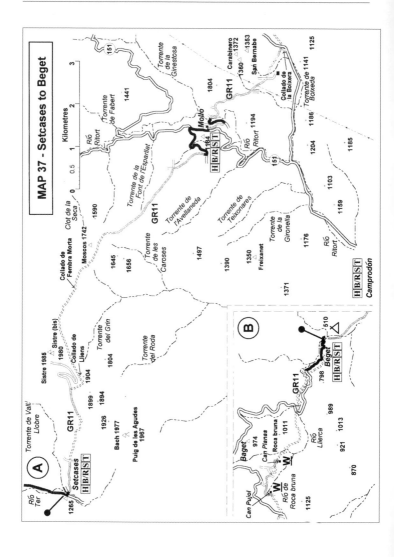

MAP 37 - Setcases to Beget

look. The steep path climbs through trees, mainly just S of E, to join with the start of a grassy pista on the other side of a stream. At the first grassy place it crosses E then continues ESE. Later at a meadow it goes steeply up, SE, to locate a path going E then S up a grassy path to another going E again. Then ESE up steep grass to a path turning northwards. At the next grass go E turning SE to climb beside a stream which is crossed beside a wire cage stone-retaining wall across the stream. Go along the pista, NE then ENE, for 8-9 minutes where, at waymarks, turn up the mountainside using the left side (true right side) of a rocky gully. The pass lies SE from here. Continue steeply upwards to the top of the gully. Here, look out for waymarks leading left, E, to a depression between two small hills at...

1.40 Collado de Lliens, 1877m. Cross the fence and contour ENE across the south slopes of Sistre. There are a number of tracks to choose from with waymarks from time to time. The trail looses a little height and the correct line used to be identified by a large quartz boulder ahead, which is still there but hidden by new trees. This is still some way before reaching the SE ridge from Sistre. Once on the ridge, or just to the right of it, go down SE, with a fence on the left, and in about 10 minutes reach...

2.05 Collado de la Fembra Morta, 1735m. The path continues SE below a high point on the ridge called Moscos, 1742m. *It would be very easy to become lost below Moscos in mist. The main ridge divides into two parts going S. The first and westerly carries the path that the GR11 has been using, only now descending S. The second soon also divides, with one branch going SE. The GR crosses E from one ridge to the other and then takes the SE branch.* As the ridge begins to turn S keep an eye out to the left for marks on posts at the fence which indicates the way through. Continue ESE 500 metres to a second fence on the other ridge. On the other side turn S with the fence on the right. 200 metres later, with the shallow lump of Puig de Sant Joan on the right, the faint track turns to the left, SE, to find a pista which is followed down the ridge. Follow all the way down SE and finally S, at a junction, for a short way to the road. Turn left down the road which turns N before crossing the stream and climbs steeply SE through...

3.20 Molló, 1184m. *Hotels, bar/restaurants, shops, telephone.* From the top of town turn left down the road NNE which goes to the main road. Turn right, S, along this road to the Hostal Francoise. Turn left immediately beyond the Hostal, going down a pista SSE. Go straight on through iron gate with 'Private' notice and follow GR11 and GR65 variant waymarks to concrete road. Turn left to the bridge over the...

3.40 Río Ritort, 1050m. Climb the pista SE on the other side ignoring turnings to the left or right. It climbs to fields and when approaching power lines keep left, SE, after crossing a stream. Ascend slightly to reach a T junction. *To the right, the farm Can Querol can be seen.* Leave the pistas and go straight on, SE, across the fields, spotting waymarks on trees, to a small stream below. Cross the stream and continue along a path SE. A few minutes later the path joins a pista to the road at...

4.30 Collado de la Boixera, 1110m. Cross the road and locate the waymarked path going down E into the wood, not the obvious pista going SE. Soon cross a stream and then turn down left, E. Do not follow the path into the field ahead. At a fallen tree turn left, NE, to soon join the pista going N passing Can Pujol, seen on the right. The pista soon turns E, avoiding a pista to the left, then turns S then E. Look out for new sign-posted way across fields to the right. Follow this track to a field and turn right to locate the path a short distance away, which joins the pista again. Turn sharp right, S, and in a few minutes arrive at...

5.05 Can Planas, 830m. Just before the main building take a pista for a short way and then a path left, SE. Follow the marks past various buildings to drop steeply down to the Camprodon-Beget road. *The Spanish guide says turn right and follow the road to Beget while showing the road in a different position on the map.* Cross the road and go down to the stream, crossing by a quaint and ancient stone bridge, and continue along the left bank of the Río Llierca. A little later cross to the right bank by another stone bridge and climb back up to the road once more. Turn either left and follow the road to the village or turn right a short distance and follow marks climbing into the wood on the opposite side of the road. This returns to the road later for about 100m before turning left down a track which avoids the last bends of the road, returning to the road for the last few metres into...

6.30 Beget, 510m. *A pretty village almost deserted outside of the holiday season. The 12th century church dedicated to Sant Cristofor, is a national monument. There is a hostal, bar/restaurants and a small shop in season. Out of season Can Joanic should be open, except Tuesdays (Tel: 972 741 241/Mobile 989-500 302), or find the bar to the NE of the village. It is possible to camp in the meadows below the houses; best ask at the bar.*

Day 38: Beget - Sant Aniol d'Aguja

Distance:	16.5 kilometres
Height gain:	690 metres
Height loss:	740 metres
Time:	4hrs 40mins

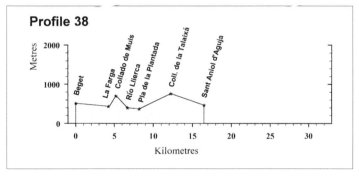

A varied route of paths and pistas arrive at the remains of the Benedictine monastery established in the 9th century. Just below Les Feixanes, I met Andrew and Meredith, two young Australians who had been walking 10 days, only seeing one pair of backpackers in that time. I had been walking 8 days and they were the first I had seen! Provisions for two days needed.

Maps: *Editorial Alpina Garrotxa. Please note that most maps show Sant Aniol d'Aguja on the wrong side of the river.*

Camping: *Below Torrente de Bellistil, and at Sant Aniol.*

0.00 Beget, 510m. From the square beside the church go S down the waymarked pista on the right of the stream. Shortly cross the

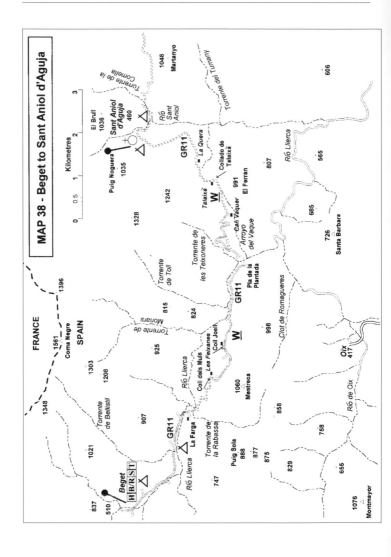

MAP 38 - Beget to Sant Aniol d'Aguja

river by a stone bridge and continue SE ignoring a pista going up left and another going right over a bridge. There are several concrete sections along this pista. Camping possible below the junction with the Torrente de Bellistil. Avoid another pista off left here. Ignore yet another, left, later but follow the pista that fords the River Llierca to reach...

0.45 La Farga, 440m. *Large inhabited building.* Below the buildings, take the marked path across the Rabassa stream and follow the path up through the trees, SSE then SE, to a pass called Coll dels Muls, 700m. Follow the path to pass through the ruined buildings ahead called...

1.30 Les Feixanes, 680m. Follow the pista down SW on the other side of the ruins. This turns SE and going down bends to the NE, passes the track to the left going to Coll Joell and then a few minutes later a spring on the right in the wood. Some minutes later ignore a pista to the left but continue following the right bank of the Río Llierca. Ten minutes later bear right at a junction, SE, and then as the valley narrows ahead keep an eye open for the waymarked path left at a meadow, with signpost on the left...

2.25 Pla de la Plantada, 370m. Turn left, E, and cross the river and pick up the trail climbing NE through the wood. Shortly it joins a pista at a bend. Go up NE and in a moment the trail takes to a path to the right climbing steeply ENE through undergrowth. If the track is overgrown, continue on the pista which also climbs steeply in places as it makes a bend to the N to join with the GR later. The path joins the pista again. Turn right and climb the pista NE and around bends to Can Vaquer. Continue by a path ENE on the left of the house and follow the marks to...

3.35 Collado de Talaixà, 760m. *A church and ruined village above on the left contains a water point. Dry in 1999.* Go down N then NE to the ruin of La Quera. Exit up left and the trail continues ENE and, having turned NNW, climbs above the crags called Salt de la Núvia. Descend then, turning NE, pass through a gate and follow the trail turning E to...

4.40 Sant Aniol d'Aguja, 460m. *Church, unlocked in 1999, with interesting cave below. The water point only flows slowly. If dry, water must be obtained from the river below, behind the church. There is an* *open fronted arch suitable for bivouac and camping in the old terraced meadows. This is a very busy place during the summer, at weekends, due to canyonning in the local rivers. Having replenished water supplies, there is a quieter field a short distance into the next day at the southern tip of El Brull.*

Day 39: Sant Aniol d'Aguja - Albanyà

Distance:	18 kilometres
Height gain:	685 metres
Height loss:	910 metres
Time:	6hrs 15mins

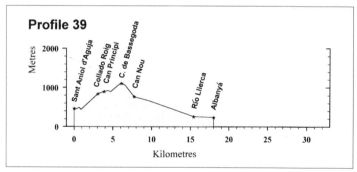

Pleasant forest trails, though not so pleasant during or after rain, lead finally to the pista at Can Nou and easy ground the long way down to Albanyá. Water will be needed to last all day, as replenishment cannot be guaranteed at either Can Galan or Can Nou, both dry in the summer of 1999.

Maps: *Editorial Alpina Garrotxa.*

Camping: *Camping Bassegoda west of Albanyà, open all year, except at Christmas. Restaurant and bar service.*

0.00 Sant Aniol d'Aguja, 460m. Follow the path down SE for about 3mins and cross the Río Sant Aniol below and on the left. Follow the path on the other side as it climbs round to the NW along the right bank of the Comella valley avoiding the path going S. The clearly marked path climbs well above the river,

La Guingueta from the narrow road to Jou (Day 25)

The GR 11 along the Núria gorge (Day 35)
The castle of Requesens with the Mediterranean in the distance (Day 42)

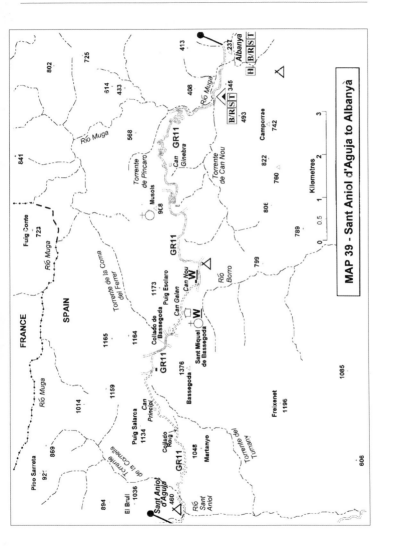

MAP 39 - Sant Aniol d'Aguja to Albanyà

which is a bit disconcerting, as one expects it to be crossing the water. However, persevere and this is what it does shortly. From the left bank of the Torrente de la Comella climb E through the trees. Signpost to Albanyà. Higher, it crosses a scree slope before reaching...

1.30 Collado Roig, 840m. Turn left NE and follow the path as it contours the slope, then climbs, passing Can Principi about 30 minutes later. Continue NW to the head of the valley where the stream bed is crossed. The trail leads steeply upward ESE for about 3 minutes to join a grassy pista SE which soon leads to a ruin on the right. Take the marked, ascending path to the left, ENE, being careful to spot two sharp left turns which access higher paths. The first is obscured by small pines and is only a short way from the ruin. Waymarks confirm the correct paths that climb to the pista above. Turn right, SE, a little later, avoiding the turning going right to Bassegoda, 1379m, to reach...

2.55 Collado de Bassegoda, 1105m. Continue across the pass for a few minutes before it descends SE ignoring two pistas to the left. About 100m from the second pista turn left, E, down a well marked path through the wood. GR11 signpost to Sant Aniol. The path zigzags steeply down passing Can Galan (Refugio de Bassegoda) over on the right. *A mountain hut with dubious bottled water and about 20 places.* Continue down to the buildings of...

4.00 Can Nou, 780m. Follow the pista E passing a water point on the left after 300m, the Fuente de Can Nou, dry in 1999, and a pista to the right a few minutes later. Much later, as the GR pista turns north once more, ignore the pista to the right and then about 10mins later, below Musols, 908m, turn sharp right, SW, at a junction. Follow the pista down as it makes a large loop back to the E again. More zigzags lead down to the Río Muga where at the T junction turn right, S, following the pista along the right bank of the river. This leads past the large and well-appointed campsite and on to cross the bridge just a few minutes from...

6.15 Albanyà, 237m. *Small village with hotel, restaurant and several bars and telephone.*

Day 40: Albanyà - La Vajol

Distance:	27 kilometres
Height gain:	860 metres
Height loss:	550 metres
Time:	6hrs 20mins

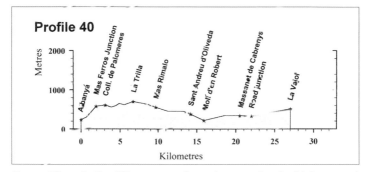

From Albanyà the GR goes northwards to maintain high ground through a nice mix of forest paths and pistas. Hopefully, with the navigation problems solved, it will be a very pleasant, though long, walk. Water supplies can be replenished just below Mas Rimalo. Please note that there are four main changes to the original route. Continental guides show the route from Albanyà ascending from the wrong road bridge. They also make a loop to pass by Mas Ferreros but it is not necessary to do this. Also, the route has been substantially changed from Molí d'en Robert, no doubt due to the rescinding of the right of way by Can Vall. On the outskirts of Massanet de Cabrenys the route to the road has moved further to the west. Provisions can be obtained by a diversion to Massanet de Cabrenys. It might be possible to acquire some trail food at the bar in La Vajol. Otherwise, La Jonquera will be the next certain place to re-provision.

Maps: *SGE 38-11 and 38-10.*

Camping: *Possibility at Molí d'en Robert and at La Vajol, at the car park at the lower end of the village. There are two fields above and to the SE. However, these both are unpleasant now, all but filled with old vehicles.*

0.00 Albanyà, 237m. Leave the town by the road to the E. At the

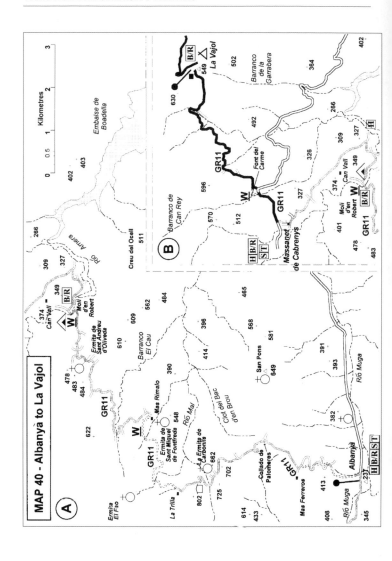

MAP 40 - Albanyà to La Vajol

edge of town, at the first bridge, turn left, N, and follow the well marked pista, at first, then footpath, which follows the right bank of the stream for a short distance before climbing steeply to the left. After about 30 minutes it comes upon a pista which is followed upwards, N, for about 2 minutes before taking a short-cut straight on N across a bend of this pista. Cross the pista and continue to climb the path N, which soon joins the pista yet again, which is followed left, NW, and on to a sharp right bend. Just after this bend turn left, N, to climb a path through the wood. This comes upon the pista again where one turns left, NW, for a short distance before reaching a junction at open ground. Slightly left the pista goes to Mas Ferreros but the GR11 turns right, NE, along an earth pista. In about 10 minutes, at a junction, this pista arrives at...

1.15 Collado de Palomeres, 605m. Take the left branch, NNW, and follow it as it contours, more or less, the slopes ahead, passing La Ermita de Carbonils seen down to the right. About 10mins later the Refugio de Seglar is seen to the left. *Private hut, locked and no water outside, but with tables under shelter.* Continue NNW to...

2.05 La Trilla, 700m. Leave the pista for a path entering the woods NE. Don't take the one going NNW. Follow the waymarks as the trail turns N then E and N and E again to cross a small stream and drop down to the ruins of Mas Rimalo. At the pista, turn left, N, signposted to Albanyà, avoiding a turning on the right. About 4mins later pass a water point on the left and continue along the pista avoiding turns to the left and then turns to the right as indicated on the sketch map. This eventually reaches the complex of...

3.40 Ermita de Sant Andreu d'Oliveda, 380m. Take the pista E and follow down to and across the stream to...

4.00 Molí d'en Robert, 220m. *Picnic area, swimming pool, bar/restaurant and small campsite in season. Nothing open except during the summer.* **NB: the route no longer leaves to the N.** Just above the buildings, turn right, SE, and follow the pista for some time before other waymarks appear. Avoid a turning left after 700m but turn left, N, at the next junction. The pista then ascends to join another a few minutes later. Turn sharp left, NW, and follow the pista N and NW to higher open farmland where, after one kilometre, the old route joins from the left. Continue NW to the edge of Massanet de Cabrenys. Avoid the concrete road going down steeply to the right, which was the old way, but continue on, following the marks past the football pitch over on the right. Turn right, N, at the first housing access road. Shortly leave the road to the right and then left to follow a path beside fields, which joins a farm pista for about 150m before joining the main road. *To the left, ESE, is Massanet de Cabrenys with all the usual services.* Turn right and follow the road for one kilometre to the Barranco de Can Rey where the road turns sharply to the south. Cross the bridge and turn left, N, following a path to...

5.15 Font del Carme, 330m. *Water point.* Turn right, E, and go up the track to join a pista, which almost immediately joins the road coming up from just beyond the bridge. Follow this road E, as it climbs generally to the NE all the way to...

6.20 La Vajol, 549m. *The pista arrives at a large restaurant above to the left. The village lies below to the right. There are two other restaurant/bars in the old village but no accommodation. There is a Hostal but it is closed. Camping in the fields is unpleasant, but possible. Water can be had from a fountain beside the Jewish memorial, at the bottom of the steps, at the southern end of the village. Enquiry might gain access to some shelter, set aside for GR11 walkers.*

Day 41: La Vajol - Requesens

Distance:	24.5 kilometres
Height gain:	830 metres
Height loss:	880 metres
Time:	6hrs 20mins

The day of the pista! Mostly on pistas, the route comes down to the large road marshalling area to the north of Jonquera to pass under the motorway into the town. Then it passes over the ridge to the east to reach Requesens. The climb over the ridge has been greatly improved by volunteers cutting back the thorn bushes that had almost overgrown the path and now it is a pleasure to use this path. Thorns beginning to encroach in 1999.

Maps: *SGE 39-10.*

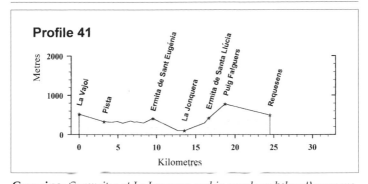

Camping: *Campsites at La Jonquera and in meadows below Requesens.*

0.00 La Vajol, 549m. Take the road from the car park going down NW which later turns E and follow for 3.3km where waymarks indicate a turn left, N, along a pista. This soon joins another coming from the right. Turn left, NW, and go along this pista which turns NE passing Mas Carreres, avoiding the turns to the left and right indicated on the sketch map, to arrive at...

1.30 Ermita de Santa Eugénia, 350m. Take the pista ESE which in about 10 minutes arrives at a junction. Turn left, NNW. A few minutes later the water point of Can Marine is passed (dry in 1999). The pista crosses a stream and begins to climb. At a junction, at the top of the hill, turn right, SE. The route continues E and in about 10 minutes turn right, SE, at another junction. The pista continues generally SE and in a further 15-20 minutes, turn right at a pista joining from the left. In another 10-15 minutes, turn SE at a junction. 10 minutes or so later, the waymarks indicate a turn left to cross a bridge over the motorway but it is better to turn right, SE, alongside a wire fence, unless the Hypermarket is required on the main road. About 15 minutes later this turns left to an underpass and to a bridge over the Río Llobregat and the centre of...

3.15 La Jonquera, 110m. *A town adjacent to the Customs check area on the motorway. All normal facilities can be found. The best supermarkets are beyond the bridge turning right, S. Sufficient provisions will be needed in order to reach Llanca, as the next re-provisioning point. Meals can probably be had at Requesens and at Sant*

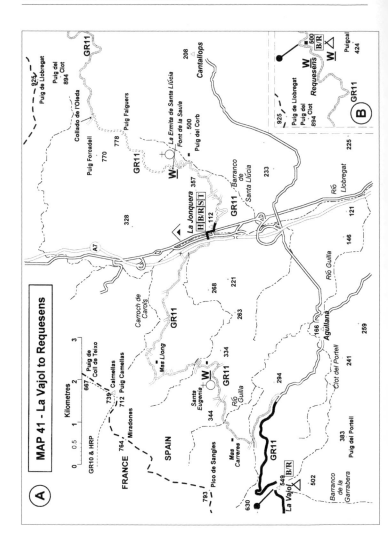

MAP 41 - La Vajol to Requesens

Quirze de Colera. Cross the bridge and turn right, S, and after some 250 metres turn left and climb steeply to the SE of town by way of Carrer Cantallops, La Placa del Sol and Carrer Jossello which leads to a pista, soon taking the left branch. New, useable, short cuts have been waymarked between various sections of the pista. Please refer to the sketch map. The pista twists and turns, generally NE, climbing the right side of the Barranco de Sant Llúcia. When in sight of Ermita de Sant Llúcia, take the path to the left, NNE, and then left again, NNW, steeply to...

4.15 Fuente de la Saula, 420m. *Fine views to the coast and the Gulf of Rosas from beside the hermitage. This has become a popular barbecue site in summer. The pista coming from the Cantallops road has been surfaced.* Go up the steps opposite the water point turning left to find waymarks leading to a clear path going NW, climbing through thorn bushes which have been cut back allowing good progress. The trail climbs generally NE now and passes just below the summit of...

5.10 Puig Falguers, 778m. Continue N passing some rocky outcrops on their western side turning NE to go down to the pista below, near to the Collado de l'Oleda, 700m. Turn right and follow the main pista down. *There is a memorial to the French aircrew lost in a DC 6 crash in 1986, just as the track steepens.* Follow the pista to the small hamlet of...

6.20 Requesens, 500m. *Popular traditional bar/restaurant. Water point on the left before reaching the buildings and another below, SW, among terraces just suitable for camping. The resident bull seems quite harmless! There is a toilet and shower behind the bar/restaurant.*

Day 42: Requesens - St. Quirze de Colera

Distance:	26 kilometres
Height gain:	575 metres
Height loss:	910 metres
Time:	6hrs 15mins

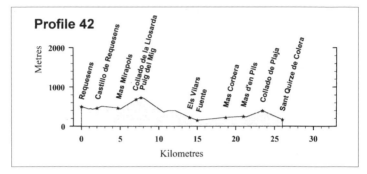

A long but gentle day with no major climbs passing mostly through open countryside. Care with navigation will only be required off pista. A lot of ground is covered due to the extent of pistas used. Excitement mounts as the coast is seen ever closer! **NB. The heat now can become a problem in summer. The only water point that can be expected to be still flowing will be below Els Vilars.**

Maps: *SGE 39-10 and 40-10.*

Camping: *At Sant Quirze de Colera.*

0.00 Requesens, 500m. From the bar, take the pista going down N passing the Fuente el Ferro and picnic area a few minutes later. The pista turns SE and in few minutes pass another on the left closed by an iron gate. A few metres later turn left from the main pista to another pista going N. This soon crosses a wooden bridge and turns to the SE. Take the right fork here which crosses another stream and climbs to the junction to Castillo de Requesens on the right. *The Castle now is open to the public for a small fee, but only opens at 10.00am.* Go straight on E with the stone wall on the right. In about 10mins turn left, N, at another junction. Follow this pista all the way to Mas Mirapols. A path

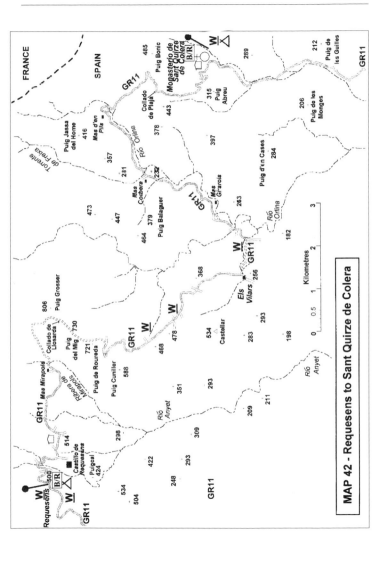

MAP 42 - Requesens to Sant Quirze de Colera

leads down NNE to Ribera de Mirapols. On the other side, the path first turns S then ENE and again turning S to reach...

1.50 Collado de Llosada, 690m. *Fine views in good weather and from various points along the top of the ridge.* The marked way continues SW on the western side of the ridge until below Puig del Mig, 730m, marks lead through a fence on the left. Take care here to find the correct route. *Once the trail went E from here but does so no longer.* Immediately after crossing the fence turn right, S, to find a clear marked path but very soon take a less distinct branch to the left, S, and the waymarks lead to the left, E, of the rocky high ground ahead, the Puig de Roureda, 721m. Follow the path down, S, to join a pista and turn right, W. Follow this pista down as it turns generally SSE ignoring various turnings. Cross a stream and ascend a little and then follow all the way to...

3.30 Els Vilars, 220m. Leave the pista for a track on the left, E, which goes down to a stream. Take care to spot the waymarks here. Cross the stream and follow a clear path SE which soon turns left along a not-so-clear path beside the stream. About 20mins from Els Vilars, this path comes to a road at the Fuente de Cadecas. *The water quality is not too good in summer. No ill effects were had though, and copious sterilised quantities were consumed later (1999).* Go straight up the narrow road which soon becomes a pista with one or two concrete sections. After about 10-12mins, waymarks indicate a path to the right, E, used as a short cut. Soon join the pista again going NE. Mas Girarols is seen off to the right. Then much later...

4.30 Mas Corbera, 215m. Seen on the left. Take the right branch of the pista which crosses the Torrente de Freixa and continues NE to Mas d'en Pils on the left. Follow the pista to the right, S, or cut across the arid fields to cross the Rio Orlina and go up the other side, generally SSE, and with a turn to the right, SW, reach the obvious pass ahead...

5.40 Collado de Plaja, 395m. Follow the pista S to the old monastery seen among the fields below. Lower down the trail makes a number of zigzags before arriving at...

6.15 Monasterio de Sant Quirze de Colera, 165m. *A new bar/restaurant, run by Luis and Christina, has opened in 1999. It may be possible to use the shower in the ladies toilet. The bothy within the* *monastery may also still be in use. If camping, there is a spring higher up to the E among the terraces. There was also a tap near to the monastery in 1999, used by renovation workmen.*

Day 43: St. Quirze de Colera - El Port de la Selva

Distance:	27 kilometres
Height gain:	775 metres
Height loss:	925 metres
Time:	6hrs 40mins

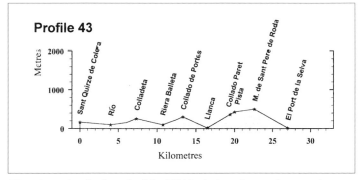

There is a sting in the tail of the GR11. As it arrives at the coast it turns south to climb nearly 500 metres to the monastery of Sant Pere de Roda. This is set on the upper north facing slopes of Roda, 670m and overlooking El Port de la Selva. The monastery is undergoing some form of restoration. There are plenty of places at Llanca in which one can refuel for the climb. This will be a long but pleasant day with views over the coast.

Maps: *SGE 40-10 and 40-11.*

Camping: *Campsites at Llanca and near to El Port de la Selva.*

0.00 Monestario de Sant Quirze de Colera, 165m. Take the obvious pista southward all the way to...

1.15 Vilamaniscle, 155m. *Good water point at the entrance to the village. No other facilities here now.* Take the second turning left, NE, which climbs steeply to the edge of town. Near the top, take a left then right to follow the signs to 'Las Casas de Colonies

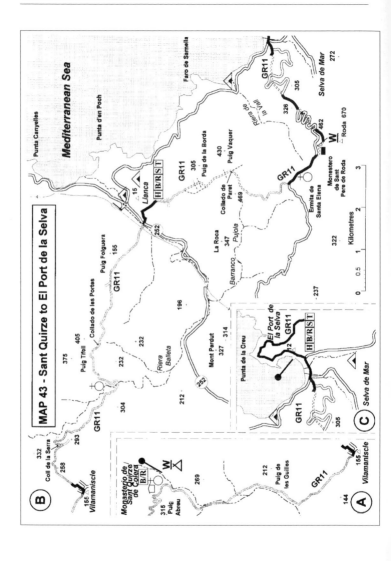

MAP 43 - Sant Quirze to El Port de la Selva

Tramuntana'. This large holiday centre is soon passed and the marks appear. Continue NE climbing to the...

1.40 Collado de la Serra, 260m. Take the pista left, N, which goes down soon turning SE, avoiding a pista to the left. Two kilometres or so later, cross the Riera Balleta. Avoid the level pista to the left which goes to the Ermita de Sant Silvestre but climb the other one going NW then NE above Sant Silvestre, with its vast area of ancient terraces now overgrown. Continue the climb to the...

2.45 Collado de les Portes, 230m. *Llanca and the sea seen to the east.* Take the left pista, E then generally ESE, all the way down to the main road. *The route no longer goes along the main road to the town but works its way through the small streets to the west.* Cross the road to waymarks and find the best way to the centre for provisions.

3.30 Llanca, 15m. *All necessary facilities.* From the centre, locate 'Carrer Nicolas Salmeron' to the west. Then first left, S, 'Carrer Nord', keeping left at a fork into 'Carrer Aforca'. Turn right at the end to see 'Carrer Sant Pere de Roda' going S. Follow this to a pista and shortly go right at a fork, then straight across at a crossing. After a streambed the pista steepens, S, and waymarks lead along a track ahead. There are various path junctions as indicated on the sketch map but this path climbs steeply to reach an obvious pass called...

4.40 Collado de Paret, 360m. Turn right, SW, and climb the steep vegetated ridge. In about 10-15mins, depending on how hot and tired you feel, the path arrives at a welcome pista. Turn left, SE, and follow to the El Port de la Selva to Vilajuiga road. Turn left, SE, and follow to the entrance of...

5.35 Monasterio de Sant Pere de Roda, 500m. Pass through the gate and walk down the new sloping apron on the north side of the monastery. *A short way down and below, on a small flat grassy platform, is a spring. Major works are still in progress in 1999.* Continue to the newly bulldozed pista and follow down to a large car parking area which looks like a very wide road when empty. Continue down to the actual road and go straight across to find a path going straight down and across the many zigzags of the road. Sketch map shows details. The last section is somewhat thorny and awkward as it passes over old terrace retaining stone walls but does save a very long section of road. Arriving at the roads and houses below of Urbanizacion Euromar, just follow the roads down to the main Llanca/El Port de la Selva road. *Turn left for 1.7 kilometres to Camping Port de la Vall, open all year, though the restaurant will only be open during the holiday season. Turn right then right again down the Cadequés road for about 1 kilometre to Camping Port de la Selva, open June to September. There is a small site just to the right and opposite but it, no doubt, will be full of water-sport campers in summer.* Turn right, ESE, along the road to...

6.40 El Port de la Selva, 12m. *Hotels, bar/restaurants, telephones and campsites nearby.*

Day 44: El Port de la Selva - Cabo de Creus

Distance:	16 kilometres
Height gain:	445 metres
Height loss:	440 metres
Time:	4hrs 20mins

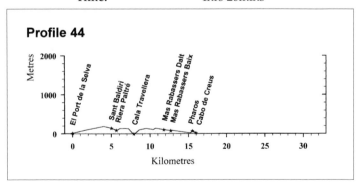

Though near to the coast, this last day still retains the GR11 ambience of remoteness. Mixed emotions too, sadness as this is the last of many days of wilderness wandering and excitement in anticipation of returning to loved ones. Water will need to be carried for the whole day.

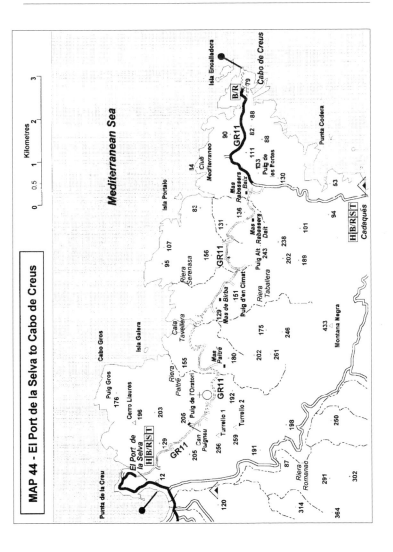

MAP 44 - El Port de la Selva to Cabo de Creus

The bar/restaurant, run by Chris Little, at Cabo Creus should be open during the summer (Tel: 972 19 90 05). He does have a room for GR11 walkers. If this is not available or not wanted, then returning from Cabo de Creus to civilisation is a problem. Perhaps the best way is to stay 2 days at El Port, travel light and retrace one's steps. There is a bus from El Port to Llanca or a pleasant coastal footpath. It is possible to walk or hitch to Cadaqués where buses go to Figueras. There is only one taxi here. Hitching back to El Port is also possible from Cadaqués, though there is a long hill to climb with most of the traffic going in the Figueras direction.

Maps: SGE 40-10 and 40-11.

Camping: *Due to the arid nature of the terrain it is not easy to camp. It may be possible to ask at one of the farms. Otherwise, there is a campsite at Port Lligat just NE of Cadaqués, if you are going that way, which is open during the summer only and has gravel pitches.*

0.00 El Port de la Selva, 12m. Follow the coast road N, the Carrer del Mar, and as it climbs the headland, marks appear. The road climbs steeply to the SE while the road down left to the Cala Tamariua is ignored. Climb steeply up the road right, S, which soon becomes a pista. A little later pass a road coming up from the right. About 10mins later the pista makes a bend to the N before returning to the SE again. In another 10mins the access road to Can Puignau is passed on the left. Continue SE and in 5mins take the left fork, SE. In about 3mins turn left, E, along a wide path and in a few minutes this comes upon a junction of pistas. Take the one going SE which in a few minutes terminates at...

1.05 Ermita de Sant Baldiri, 140m. Continue along the path ESE which curves around to the dry stream bed of Riera Paltré where it turns left, N, to join with the pista coming from the right. Turn left, NW, along the pista which turns to the E. About 12mins along this pista fork left, N, and then shortly WNW, along a path which turns to the E to go down steeply over rocky ground to...

1.55 Cala Tavellera, 0m. *There is a fisherman's hut on the left. While here in 1999 it appeared as if a new route was being set up. The waymark across the bay had disappeared and others on the climb out had been partly over-painted. Waymarks appeared later, as expected,*

The stone seat and the end

but no other way was found. A few hundred metres past the 'tree' workmen were erecting an iron gate with danger warning sign for anyone coming from the other direction. Cross the pebbles to the ascending track on the other side of the bay. Climb the path to join a pista going SE. 10 minutes or so later, take the left, SE, branch and a few minutes later the pista joins another below a pylon. Follow this pista, N, which turns to the NE. In a few minutes this reaches a solitary pine. Turn right, E, continuing along the pista. About 7 minutes later, at a junction, turn right, S, and follow the pista as it makes a turn to the N, passing the aforementioned gate, before returning to the SE. Sometime later it passes the ruined Mas Rabassers Dalt, seen to the right, turning to the E to reach...

3.10 Mas Rabassers Baix, 75m. The pista joins another crossing at right angles. Cross the grass straight ahead, E, and follow the marks to climb up to the road in a few minutes. Turn left, E, and ascend the road and follow, undulating, past the left turn to the Club Mediterraneo and on to the neck of the final peninsula. Take the narrow steep cobbled path that climbs spectacularly across the south face of the cliff to reach the lighthouse area. Waymarks lead down E to a stone built bench overlooking the sea and Isla Masa de Oro at...

4.20 Cabo de Creus, 15m. *The bar/ restaurant is now open all year. See above for return suggestions. There is a bus from Cadaqués to Figueras that leaves just after 5pm. In Figueras there is an HI hostal on the west of town and a campsite 3 kilometres to the NNW, which is poor but with a restaurant which is excellent. All other services here, too. There is also a bus from Cadaqués to El Port but this is only of use if staying overnight in Cadaqués.*

GR11 VARIANTS

SHORT NOTES ON ALTERNATIVE OR ACCESS ROUTES

I have not always followed the official main route as some variants have become the better way and are the most popular. Not all variants have acquired an individual route suffix but where these are attributed, they have been noted.

Variant No.1. GR11.1 Selba d'Oza to Candanchú via Refugio de Lizara (Commencing Day 11). Two days are required with a stop-over at the Refugio de Lizara. Go S to the Puen de Santa Ana, 920m. Then E to the Refugio de Lizara, 1540m. Continue E to Collado d'o Boxo, 2019m. Then SE to Collado de Riguelo, 2043m. SE to Canfranc and then N, using the GR65.3 variant, to join either the GR11 main route or the Collado de Izas variant.

Variant No.2. GR11 Candanchú to Sallent de Gállego via Cuello d'Izas (Day 12). Leave the main route at the Canal Roya entrance, going S then E into the Canal d'Izas and on to the Cuello d'Izas, 2230m. Go down NE and then ENE by pista, turning N along a path to join with the Canal Roya route just before the turning to Formigal.

Variant No.3. GR11 Góriz to Pineta via the Cuello d'Añisclo (Day 16). This is described in the text for Day 16.

Variant No.4. GR11.2 Circuit of the three refugios (Commencing Day 19). Two days required. Just past the Refugio de Viadós turn right, S then SE, beside the Barranco de la Ribereta to the Collado de Eriste or, Collado de Forqueta, 2860m. Go down E to the Refugio d'Angel Orus or Refugio d'el Forcau, 2095m. The next day go N then E to the Collada de la Pllana, 2702m. Go down E to the Ibón Pequeño de Batisielles, 1960m. From here go E across a little pass, then NNE and some time later NW, down to the Refugio d'Estós, 1890m.

Variant No.5. GR11 Collado de Vallibierna to Refugio de Llausét (Day 21). Go down SE from the pass to the junction at 2410m. Turn right, S, and then pass along the northern shore of Ibón de Llausét, 2200m. Turn S then SE to the Refugio de Llausét, 1940m.

Variant No.6. GR11 Access from the small village of Aneto to Refugio de Llausét (Access to Day 21). Leave the village by the road going SW. A steep short cut across a loop in the road leads to a trail, E, around the south ridge of Pic del Home and above the road. This joins the road eventually for a further kilometre. Then a track is taken around the head of the valley to reach the Refugio de Llausét to the E.

Variant No.7. GR11 Refugio de Llausét to Refugio d'Anglós (part of the access from Aneto to the main route). Go NW to the Ibón de Llausét passing N along its E side. Turn right, at a small tunnel mouth, to climb NNE to the Collado d'Anglós, 2429m. Go down E then NE to join with the main route just before the Refugio d'Anglós, 2220m.

Variant No.8. GR11 Refugio de la Restanca to Refugio de Colomers via Pont de Rius (Day 23). The main route in this guide is designated GR11.18. Cross the dam and go down the wide track, N, to the Pont de Rius, 1700m. Take the pista NE for just under 3km, where a right branch is taken which climbs SE to the lake Basa de Montcasau, 1940m. Continue by a path to the Port de la Ribereta, 2350m. After some descent go over another smaller pass, 2238m, and then down, S, to join with the main route just W of the Refugio de Colomers, 2115m.

Variant No.9. GR11.20 Pont de Suert to Espot via Boi, Refugio de Colomina, Collado de Saburo and Refugio Josep Maria Blanc (Access to Day 25). Three days are required. There is a road that gives access to Boi and Taull but the GR11 takes a twisting route above the road and some 1 to 3km to the E. It goes in a NE direction with a long detour to the W around Serrahis, 1585m. It continues NE to Boi and then E to Taull to complete the first day. There is accommodation at Boi. Three kilometres of road SE from Taull lead to a path continuing SE to Port de Rus, 2627m. Go down zigzags, E, to the Barranc de Rus, following the valley down ENE. Go up the valley opposite to climb to the Collada de Font Sobirana, 2425m. From there continue generally NE and over another small pass to reach the Refugio de Colomina, 2396m, and the end of the second day. Continue NE to the Collado de Saburó, 2670m, then down NE past the Refugio J.M.

Blanc, 2364m. Follow the delightful Peguera valley down to Espot, 1320m.

Variant No.10. GR11.10 Les Escaldes to Cabana dels Esparvers via Refugio Cap del Rec (Day 31). Two days are required. The GR7 is taken SE from Les Escaldes which lies a few kilometres S from Encamp down the main road. In about 50mins take the right branch which climbs SSE to the Port de Perafita, 2570m. Pass into Spain and continue down SE and then generally ESE to reach the Refugio Cap del Rec, 1980m. E then SSE to Viliella before turning N beside the Riu de la Llosa to Cabana dels Esparvers, 2068m.

Variant No.11. GR11.8 Dórria to Planoles via Fornells de la Muntanya (Day 34). Follow the road S then W from Dórria to join with the main road below. Turn right, W then S, for 3mins before taking the turning SE then WSW to Fornells de la Muntanya, 1284m. Take the pista going E, to the S of the railway track. Cross to the N side, some time later, to enter Planés, 1180m, and the main route of the GR11. Continue to Planoles, 1137m.

BIBLIOGRAPHY

Classic Walks in the Pyrenees - Kev Reynolds - The Oxford Illustrated Press

GR11 Senderos de Gran Recorrido - Various - Prames S.A. (Recommended for maps)

GR11 Senders de Gran Recorregut No.1 - Various - Publicaciones del'Abadia de Montserrat S.A.

GR11 Senders de Gran Recorregut No.2 - Various

Pyrenees High Level Route - Georges Veron - Gastons-West Col Publications

La Senda, Grande Traversee des Pyrenées Espagnoles par le GR11 - Jean François Rodriguez - Rando Editions

Senda Pyrenaica, Topoguia del Sendero Aragones - Various - FAM

The Pyrenean Trail GR10 - Alan Castle - Cicerone Press

The Pyrenees, The Rough Guide - Marc Dubin - Rough Guides

Walks and Climbs in the Pyrenees - Kev Reynolds - Cicerone Press

ROUTE SUMMARY

DAY	STAGE	HEIGHT GAIN	LOSS	TIME	DIST.	ACC DIST.
1	Cabo Higuer - Vera de Bidasoa	830m	820m	6hrs 40mins	30.3km	30.3km
2	Vera Bidasoa - Elizondo	1130m	985m	7hrs 15mins	30km	60.3km
3	Elizondo - Puerto de Urkiaga	1050m	340m	5hrs 35mins	19km	79.3km
4	Puerto de Urkiaga - Burguete	680m	695m	5hrs 5mins	16km	95.3km
5	Burguete - Fábrica de Orbaiceta	600m	660m	5hrs	20.5km	115.8km
6	Fábrica de Orbaiceta - Casas de Irati	400m	380m	4hrs 10mins	16.5km	132.3km
7	Casas de Irati - Ochagavia	670m	760m	4hrs 35mins	16km	148.3km
8	Ochagavia - Isaba	710m	655m	5hrs 35mins	23.8km	172.1km
9	Isaba - Zuriza	1300m	890m	6hrs 30mins	18.5km	190.6km
10	Zuriza - Selba d'Oza	735m	825m	4hrs 40mins	15km	205.6km
11	Selba d'Oza - Candanchú	1080m	670m	6hrs 25mins	25km	230.6km
12	Candanchú - Sallent de Gállego	880m	1125m	6hrs 10mins	22.3km	252.9km
13	Sallent de Gállego - Balneario de Panticosa	1520m	1185m	9hrs	24km	276.9km
14	Balneario de Panticosa - San Nicholás de Bujaruelo	940m	1240m	6hrs 50mins	19.5km	296.4km
	Ref. de Góriz	1130m	310m	5hrs 45mins	22km	318.4km
16	Ref. de Góriz - Circo de Pineta	880m	1750m	7hrs 10mins	13.5km	331.9km
16	variant Ref. de Góriz - Circo de Pineta	590m	1460m	6hrs 40mins	11.5km	
17	Circo de Pineta - Parzán	880m	1025m	5hrs 25mins	18km	349.9km
18	Parzán - Viadós	1445m	850m	6hrs	19.5km	369.4km
19	Viadós - Ref. d'Estós	860m	710m	4hrs 15mins	11.5km	380.9km
20	Estós - Ref. del Puente de Coronas	740m	650m	5hrs 10mins	18.5km	399.4km
21	Puente de Coronas - Hospital de Viella	1070m	1420m	7hrs 45mins	19.5km	418.9km
22	Hospital de Viella - Ref. de la Restanca	770m	390m	4hrs 10mins	10.5km	429.4km
23	Ref. de la Restanca - Ref. de Colomers	660m	555m	3hrs 40mins	7.5km	436.9km

DAY	STAGE	HEIGHT		TIME	DIST.	ACC
		GAIN	LOSS			DIST.
24	Ref. de Colomers - Espot	500m	1295m	6hrs	19.5km	456.4km
25	Espot - Estaon	1500m	1580m	7hrs 30mins	20km	476.4km
26	Estaon - Tavascan	630m	750m	4hrs 20mins	12.5km	488.9km
27	Tavascan - Àreu	1120m	1015m	6hrs 20mins	17.5km	506.4km
28	Àreu - Ref. de Baiau (J.M. Montfort)	1350m	60m	5hrs 30mins	15.5km	521.9km
29	Ref. de Baiau - Arans	750m	1905m	6hrs 10mins	15km	536.9km
30	Arans - Encamp	1010m	1090m	4hrs 45mins	14.5km	551.4km
31	Encamp - Cabana dels Esparvers	1350m	560m	6hrs	20.5km	571.9km
32	C. dels Esparvers - Ref. de Malniu	810m	740m	4hrs	10.3km	582.2km
33	Ref. de Malniu - Puigcerdà	95m	1030m	3hrs 20mins	15km	597.2km
34	Puigcerdà - Planoles	1020m	1085m	7hrs	26.5km	623.7km
35	Planoles - Núria	1600m	770m	6hrs 30mins	21km	644.7km
36	Núria - Setcases	1080m	1770m	6hrs 20mins	21km	665.7km
37	Setcases - Beget	820m	1575m	6hrs 30mins	22km	687.7km
38	Beget - Sant Aniol d'Aguja	690m	740m	4hrs 40mins	16.5km	704.2km
39	Sant Aniol d'Aguja - Albanyà	685m	910m	6hrs 15mins	18km	722.2km
40	Albanyà - La Vajol	860m	550m	6hrs 55mins	27km	749.2km
41	La Vajol - Requesens	830m	880m	6hrs 20mins	24.5km	773.7km
42	Requesens - Sant Quirze de Colera	575m	910m	6hrs 15mins	26km	799.7km
43	Sant Quirze de Colera - El Port de la Selva	775m	925m	6hrs 40mins	27km	826.7km
44	El Port de la Selva - Cabo de Creus	445m	440m	4hrs 20mins	16km	842.7km

CICERONE GUIDES

WALKING AND TREKKING IN THE ALPS

WALKING IN THE ALPS *Kev Reynolds* The popular author of many of our Alpine guide-books now draws on his vast experience to produce an outstanding comprehensive volume. Every area covered. Not for over half a century has there been anything remotely comparable. Fully illustrated. *ISBN 1 85284 261 X Large format Case bound 496pp*

CHAMONIX TO ZERMATT - The Walker's Haute Route *Kev Reynolds* The classic walk in the shadow of great peaks from Mont Blanc to the Matterhorn. In 14 stages, this is one of the most beautiful LD paths in Europe. *ISBN 1 85284 215 6 176pp*

THE GRAND TOUR OF MONTE ROSA *C.J. Wright*

Vol 1: - MARTIGNY TO VALLE DELLA SESIA (via the Italian valleys) *ISBN 1 85284 177 X 216pp*

Vol 2: - VALLE DELLA SESIA TO MARTIGNY (via the Swiss valleys) *ISBN 1 85284 178 8 182pp* The ultimate alpine LD walk which encircles most of the Pennine Alps.

TOUR OF MONT BLANC *Andrew Harper* One of the world's best walks - the circumnavigation of the Mont Blanc massif. 120 miles of pure magic, split into 11 sections. Reprinted and updated. *ISBN 1 85284 240 7 144pp PVC cover*

100 HUT WALKS IN THE ALPS *Kev Reynolds* 100 walks amid dramatic mountain scenery to high mountain huts, each with a map, photograph and route description. A fine introduction to Europe's highest mountains in France, Italy, Switzerland, Austria and Slovenia. *ISBN 1 85284 297 0 256pp*

FRANCE, BELGIUM AND LUXEMBOURG

WALKING IN THE ARDENNES *Alan Castle* 53 circular walks in this attractive area of gorges and deep cut wooded valleys, caves, castles and hundreds of walking trails. Easily accessible from the channel. *ISBN 1 85284 213 X 312pp*

SELECTED ROCK CLIMBS IN BELGIUM AND LUXEMBOURG *Chris Craggs* Perfect rock, good protection and not too hot to climb in summer. *ISBN 1 85284 155 9 188p A5*

THE BRITTANY COASTAL PATH *Alan Castle* The GR34, 360 miles, takes a month to walk. Easy access from UK means it can be split into several holidays. *ISBN 1 85284 185 0 296pp*

CHAMONIX - MONT BLANC - A Walking Guide *Martin Collins* In the dominating presence of Europe's highest mountain, the scenery is exceptional. A comprehensive guide to the area. *ISBN 1 85284 009 9 192pp PVC cover*

THE CORSICAN HIGH LEVEL ROUTE - Walking the GR20 *Alan Castle* The most challenging of the French LD paths - across the rocky spine of Corsica. *ISBN 1 85284 100 1 TOP New edition expected autumn 2000*

WALKING THE FRENCH ALPS: GR5 *Martin Collins* The popular trail from Lake Geneva to Nice. Split into stages, each of which could form the basis of a good holiday. *ISBN 1 85284 051 X 160pp*

WALKING THE FRENCH GORGES *Alan Castle* 320 miles through Provence and Ardèche, includes the famous gorges of the Verdon. *ISBN 1 85284 114 1 224pp*

FRENCH ROCK *Bill Birkett* THE guide to many exciting French crags! Masses of photo topos, with selected hit-routes in detail. *ISBN 1 85284 113 3. 332pp A5 size*

WALKING IN THE HAUTE SAVOIE *Janette Norton* 61 walks in the pre-Alps of Chablais, to majestic peaks in the Faucigny, Haut Giffre and Lake Annecy regions. *ISBN 1 85284 196 6 312pp*

TOUR OF THE OISANS: GR54 *Andrew Harper* This popular walk around the Dauphiné massif and Écrins national park is similar in quality to the celebrated Tour of Mont Blanc. A two week suggested itinerary covers the 270km route. *ISBN 1 85284 157 5 120pp PVC cover*

TOUR OF MONT BLANC *see WALKING AND TREKKING IN THE ALPS, above*

WALKING IN PROVENCE *Janette Norton* 42 walks through the great variety of Provence - remote plateaux, leafy gorges, ancient villages, monuments, quiet towns. Provence is evocative of a gentler life. *ISBN 1 85284 293 8 248pp*

THE PYRENEAN TRAIL: GR10 *Alan Castle* From the Atlantic to the Mediterranean at a lower level than the Pyrenean High Route. 50 days but splits into holiday sections. *ISBN 1 85284 245 8 176pp*

WALKS AND CLIMBS IN THE PYRENEES *Kev Reynolds See entry under FRANCE/SPAIN*

THE TOUR OF THE QUEYRAS *Alan Castle* A 13 day walk which traverses wild but beautiful country, the sunniest part of the French Alps. Suitable for a first Alpine visit. *ISBN 1 85284 048 X 160pp*

THE ROBERT LOUIS STEVENSON TRAIL *Alan Castle* 140 mile trail in the footsteps of Stevenson's Travels with a Donkey through the Cevennes, from Le Puy to St Jean du Gard. This route is ideal for people new to walking holidays. *ISBN 1 85284 060 9 160pp*

ROCK CLIMBS IN THE PYRENEES *Derek Walker See entry under FRANCE/SPAIN*

WALKING IN THE TARENTAISE AND BEAUFORTAIN ALPS *J.W. Akitt* The delectable mountain area south of Mont Blanc includes the Vanoise National Park. 53 day walks, 5 tours between 2 and 8 day's duration, plus 43 short outings. *ISBN 1 85284 181 8 216pp*

ROCK CLIMBS IN THE VERDON - An Introduction *Rick Newcombe* An English-style guide, which makes for easier identification of the routes and descents. *ISBN 1 85284 015 3 72pp*

TOUR OF THE VANOISE *Kev Reynolds* A 10-12 day circuit of one of the finest mountain areas of France, between Mt. Blanc and the Écrins. The second most popular mountain tour after the Tour of Mont Blanc. *ISBN 1 85284 224 5 120pp*

WALKS IN VOLCANO COUNTRY *Alan Castle* Two LD walks in Central France, the High Auvergne and Tour of the Velay, in a unique landscape of extinct volcanoes. *ISBN 1 85284 092 7 208pp*

THE WAY OF ST JAMES *Two titles - see FRANCE/SPAIN*

FRANCE/SPAIN

ROCK CLIMBS IN THE PYRENEES *Derek Walker* Includes Pic du Midi d'Ossau and the Vignemale in France, and the Ordesa Canyon and Riglos in Spain. *ISBN 1 85284 039 0 168pp PVC cover*

WALKS AND CLIMBS IN THE PYRENEES *Kev Reynolds* Includes the Pyrenean High Level Route. Invaluable for any backpacker or mountaineer who plans to visit this still unspoilt mountain range. (3rd Edition) *ISBN 1 85284 133 8 328pp PVC cover*

THE WAY OF ST JAMES: Le Puy to Santiago - A Cyclist's Guide *John Higginson* A guide for touring cyclists follows as closely as possible the original route but avoids the almost unrideable sections of the walkers' way. On surfaced lanes and roads. *ISBN 1 85284 274 1 112pp*

THE WAY OF ST JAMES: Le Puy to Santiago - A Walker's Guide *Alison Raju* A walker's guide to the ancient route of pilgrimage. Plus the continuation to Finisterre. *ISBN 1 85284 271 7 264pp*

SPAIN AND PORTUGAL

WALKING IN THE ALGARVE *June Parker* The author of Walking in Mallorca turns her expert attention to the Algarve, with a selection of walks to help the visitor explore the true countryside. *ISBN 1 85284 173 7 168pp*

ANDALUSIAN ROCK CLIMBS *Chris Craggs* El Chorro and El Torcal are world famous. Includes Tenerife. *ISBN 1 85284 109 5 168pp*

COSTA BLANCA ROCK *Chris Craggs* Over 1500 routes on over 40 crags, many for the first time in English. The most comprehensive guide to the area. *ISBN 1 85284 241 5 264p*

MOUNTAIN WALKS ON THE COSTA BLANCA *Bob Stansfield* An easily accessible winter walking paradise to rival Mallorca. With rugged limestone peaks and warm climate. This guide includes the 150 km Costa Blanca Mountain Way. *ISBN1 85284 165 232pp*

ROCK CLIMBS IN MAJORCA, IBIZA AND TENERIFE *Chris Craggs* Holiday island cragging at its best. *ISBN 1 85284 189 3 240pp*

WALKING IN MALLORCA *June Parker.* The 3rd edition of this great classic guide, takes account of rapidly changing conditions. Revised reprint for 1999. *ISBN 1 85284 250 4 288pp PVC cover*

BIRDWATCHING IN MALLORCA *Ken Stoba* A complete guide to what to see and where to see it. *ISBN 1 85284 053 6 108pp*

THE MOUNTAINS OF CENTRAL SPAIN *Jaqueline Oglesby* Walks and scrambles in the Sierras de Gredos and Guadarrama which rise to 2600m and remain snow capped for 5 months of the year. *ISBN 1 85284 203 2 312p*

ROCK CLIMBS IN THE PYRENEES *Derek Walker See entry under FRANCE/SPAIN*

WALKING IN THE SIERRA NEVADA *Andy Walmsley* Spain's highest mountain range is a wonderland for the traveller and wilderness backpacker alike. Mountain bike routes indicated. *ISBN 1 85284 194 X 160pp*

WALKS AND CLIMBS IN THE PICOS DE EUROPA *Robin Walker* A definitive guide to these unique mountains. Walks and rock climbs of all grades. *ISBN 1 85284 033 1 232pp PVC cover*

SWITZERLAND - including parts of France and Italy

ALPINE PASS ROUTE, SWITZERLAND *Kev Reynolds* Over 15 passes along the northern edge of the Alps, past the Eiger, Jungfrau and many other renowned peaks. A 325 km route in 15 suggested stages. *ISBN 1 85284 069 2 176pp*

THE BERNESE ALPS, SWITZERLAND *Kev Reynolds* Walks around Grindelwald, Lauterbrunnen and Kandersteg dominated by the great peaks of the Oberland. *ISBN 1 85284 243 1 248pp PVC cover*

CENTRAL SWITZERLAND - A Walking Guide *Kev Reynolds* A little known but delightful area stretching from Luzern to the St Gotthard, includes Engelberg and Klausen Pass. *ISBN 1 85284 131 1 216pp PVC cover*

CHAMONIX TO ZERMATT - *see entry under WALKING AND TREKKING IN THE ALPS*

THE GRAND TOUR OF MONTE ROSA Vols 1 & 2 *See entry under WALKING AND TREKKING IN THE ALPS*

WALKS IN THE ENGADINE, SWITZERLAND *Kev Heynolds* The superb region to the south-east of Switzerland of the Bregaglia, Bernina Alps, and the Engadine National Park. *ISBN 1 85284 003 X 192pp PVC cover*

THE JURA: WALKING THE HIGH ROUTE *Kev Reynolds* and **WINTER SKI TRAVERSES** *R. Brian Evans.* The High Route is a long distance path along the highest crest of the Swiss Jura. In winter it is a paradise for cross-country skiers. Both sections in one volume. *ISBN 1 85284 010 2 192pp*

WALKING IN TICINO, SWITZERLAND *Kev Reynolds* Walks in the lovely Italian part of Switzerland, little known to British walkers. *ISBN 1 85284 098 6 184pp PVC cover*
THE VALAIS, SWITZERLAND - A Walking Guide *Kev Reynolds* The splendid scenery of the Pennine Alps, with such peaks as the Matterhorn, Dent Blanche, and Mont Rosa providing a perfect background. *ISBN 1 85284 151 6 224pp PVC cover*

ITALY AND SLOVENIA

ALTA VIA - HIGH LEVEL WALKS IN THE DOLOMITES *Martin Collins* A guide to some of the most popular mountain paths in Europe - Alta Via 1 and 2. *ISDN 0 902363 75 1 160pp PVC cover*
THE CENTRAL APENNINES OF ITALY - Walks, Scrambles and Climbs *Stephen Fox* The mountain spine of Italy, with secluded walks, rock climbs and scrambles on the Gran Sasso d'Italia and some of Italy's finest sport climbing crags. *ISBN 1 85284 219 9 152pp*
WALKING IN THE CENTRAL ITALIAN ALPS *Gillian Price* The Vinschgau, Ortler and Adamello regions. Little known to British walkers, certain to become popular. *ISBN 1 85284 183 4 230pp PVC cover*
WALKING IN THE DOLOMITES *Gillian Price* A comprehensive selection of walks amongst spectacular rock scenery. By far the best English guide to the area. *ISBN 1 85284 079 X PVC cover*
WALKING IN ITALY'S GRAN PARADISO *Gillian Price* Rugged mountains and desolate valleys with a huge variety of wildlife. Walks from short strolls to full-scale traverses. *ISBN 1 85284 231 8 200pp*
LONG DISTANCE WALKS IN THE GRAN PARADISO *J.W. Akitt* Includes Southern Valdotain. Supplements our Gran Paradiso guide by Gillian Price. Describes Alta Via 2 and the Grand Traverse of Gran Paradiso and some shorter walks. *ISBN 1 85284 247 4 168pp*
THE GRAND TOUR OF MONTE ROSA *C.J. Wright*
See entry under WALKING AND TREKKING IN THE ALPS

ITALIAN ROCK - Selected Climbs in Northern Italy *Al Churcher.* Val d'Orco and Mello, Lecco and Finale etc. A good introduction to some great crags. *ISBN 0 902363 93 X 200pp PVC cover*
WALKS IN THE JULIAN ALPS *Simon Brown* Slovenia contains some of Europe's most attractive mountain limestone scenery. 30 walks as an introduction to the area, from valley strolls to high mountain scrambles. *ISBN 1 85284 125 7 184pp*
WALKING IN TUSCANY *Gillian Price* 50 itineraries from brief strolls to multi-day treks in Tuscany, Umbria and Latium. *ISBN 1 85284 268 7 312pp*
VIA FERRATA SCRAMBLES IN THE DOLOMITES *Höfler/Werner Translated by Cecil Davies* The most exciting walks in the world. Wires, stemples and ladders enable the 'walker' to enter the climber's vertical environment. *ISBN 1 85284 089 7 248pp PVC cover*

HIMALAYA

ADVENTURE TREKS IN NEPAL *Bill O'Connor*
ISBN 1 85223 306 0 160pp large format

ANNAPURNA - A Trekker's Guide *Kev Reynolds* Includes Annapurna Circuit, the Annapurna Sanctuary and the Pilgrim's Trail, with lots of good advice. *ISBN 1 85284 132 X 184pp*

EVEREST - A Trekker's Guide *Kev Reynolds* A new second edition of this guide to the most popular trekking region in the Himalaya. Lodges, tea-house, permits, health - all are dealt with in this indispensible guide. With updated information, clear mapping and superb photography, including detailed descriptions of approach routes from both Nepal and Tibet. *ISBN 1 85284 306 3 184pp*

GARHWAL AND KUMAON - A Trekker's and Visitor's Guide *K.P. Sharma* Almost at the centre of the Himalayan chain culminating in Nanda Devi. Garhwal consists of rugged mountains and valleys, Kumaon is more gentle. *ISBN 1 85284 264 4 200pp*

KANGCHENJUNGA - A Trekker's Guide *Kev Reynolds* Known as the Five Treasures of the Snows because of its five summits, Kangchenjunga is the world's third highest peak (8586m). The trek to base camp is regarded by many as the most beautiful walk in the world. Various options are described by one of the best of current guide book writers. *ISBN 1 85284 280 6 184pp*

LANGTANG, GOSAINKUND & HELAMBU - A Trekker's Guide *Kev Reynolds* Popular area, easily accessible from Kathmandu. *ISBN 1 85284 207 5*

Printed and bound by The Cromwell Press,